THE

Complete
Perfectionist

CURRENCY

DOUBLEDAY

New York   London   Toronto   Sydney   Auckland

For more on currency and its resources see information at the back of this book

Juan Ramón Jiménez

\\\||//

THE
Complete
Perfectionist

A Poetics of Work

\\\||//

Edited and translated by Christopher Maurer

A CURRENCY BOOK
PUBLISHED BY DOUBLEDAY
a division of Bantam Doubleday Dell Publishing Group, Inc.
1540 Broadway, New York, New York 10036

CURRENCY and DOUBLEDAY are trademarks of Doubleday, a division of
Bantam Doubleday Dell Publishing Group, Inc.

Book design by Chris Welch

English translation of two poems by Juan Ramón Jiménez from *American
Poetry: Wildness and Domesticity* by Robert Bly, copyright © 1990 by Robert
Bly. Reprinted by permission of HarperCollins Publishers, Inc.

Library of Congress Cataloging-in-Publication Data
Jiménez, Juan Ramón, 1881–1958.
The complete perfectionist : a poetics of work / Juan Ramón
Jiménez ; edited and translated by Christopher Maurer.
p.   cm.
1. Work.   2. Perfection.   3. Jiménez, Juan Ramón, 1881–1958.
I. Maurer, Christopher.   II. Title.
BJ1498.J55   1997
861'.62 — dc20   96-41684
CIP

ISBN 0-385-48022-9

FOR DANNY AND PABLO

Acknowledgments

Warm thanks for their help—and a grateful curse for their perfectionism!—to Jennifer Breheny, Lisa Brancaccio, and Harriet Rubin of Currency Doubleday. Thanks also to Bob Daniels, most attentive of copy editors; and to Francisco H.-Pinzón Jiménez for authorizing this book. I am grateful to the late Antonio Sánchez Romeralo for his impeccable edition of Juan Ramón's complete aphorisms. Deepest thanks to María Estrella Iglesias.

C.M.

Contents

CONTENTS

Introduction

From the printer, a long-awaited package: the first copies of one of his books. Fine paper, clear type, ample margins. Near the title page is a gracefully drawn sprig of parsley—his emblem of simplicity and idealism. He has written and designed the entire book in a dream of poetical and typographical perfection: "naked" poetry in the simplest, most elegant of forms.

Before others have read it, perhaps even before they have cut its pages, one of those copies lies in ruins. Torn from its binding, it lies on a table crowded with his papers. Here and there a title has been replaced with a better one, a line of verse has been canceled, a margin is bristling with notes.

"When I publish a book I'm never happy," he explains. "On the contrary, the moment I receive the first printed copy . . . I tear off the cover and begin all over again. Letting go of a book is always, for me, a provisional solution, reached on a day of weakness."

He is, unmistakably, a perfectionist. He is Juan Ramón Jiménez (1881–1958), the "complete perfectionist" of our title: maker of deathless poems and aphorisms; master of several generations of Spanish poets; winner of a Nobel Prize for Literature.

Few writers have ever yearned more intensely for perfection, defined it more carefully, or spoken so lucidly of their struggle to achieve it, one day after another, over an entire lifetime. In these pages, drawn from several of his books, Juan Ramón's thought reaches beyond ordinary notions of "quality" or "excellence." It reaches from the work of poetry to what he calls "the poetry of work": work so stunningly *right,* so instinct with surprise and beauty, that it strikes us as "fatal" and perfect.

The Complete Perfectionist is addressed not only to poets and writers but to those who dream of perfect work: professionals, artists, or craftsmen who work freely and contentedly with hands and intellect. In it I have gathered into a poetics—a system of guiding principles—the thought of a master poet and master worker. One by one, Juan Ramón takes up the most radical elements of work: time and rhythm, noise and silence, the power to remember, the ability to forget. He teaches us to live contentedly within the present; listen more attentively to instinct; draw new strength from dream and reverie; measure our work against the quiet, steady work of nature; and calm the fear of death with trust in our daily labor.

He gives us a new vision of perfection, not as an abstract, distant goal, and not as the absence of defects, but as an "endless fervor" that enlivens the hourly and daily course of our work. For Juan Ramón, perfection is always a matter of *becoming*. It lies not in the past but in the present; never in what he has done, and always in what he is doing. It is more of a path than a goal; the process of making rather than the thing made. Perfection is "ecstasy" and restless movement. It can only be caught "in motion" and "in progress."

Our path, our movement toward perfection is our work, for it is through love for our work that we can try, each day, to bring the ideal—the perfect—within reach of our eyes and hands. "Why shouldn't I love, adore, feel reverence for my work if it is the most enduring and loveliest body that I can possibly make for my soul?"

Juan Ramón's vision of perfection arose from sixty years of experience as a careful maker of poems. "Let us think more with our hands!" he once wrote. But it is also a proudly idealistic vision. Juan Ramón believes that "mankind has become excessively realistic," that "life and death are *not* what we read about in the newspapers," and that we need our impossible ideals—especially our dream of perfect work—the way we need air or water.

How close to the soul
is all that is still immensely far
from our hands!

In poetry and work, he pursues the pure essences of things, and few people have ever lived more confidently in the realm of desire and imagination.

It seems more logical to live so-called reality than so-called dream and fantasy. But at death more truth and life remains of those who lived their dream, than of those who chased reality.

In the arduous daily work of his poetry—his "discipline and oasis," his "caprice and crucible"—he cannot help looking beyond the freshly printed book in his hands, the pages awaiting revision on his table: "I want to look at things, but only see through them." In all that he looks at lies something infinitely better.

Beyond the Ivory Tower

His dream of perfect work was nurtured in solitude, but through it he hoped to leave a lasting effect on literature and on all of society. His life and work revolved around this axiom: good work, like good poetry, is "contagious." It begins in a quiet room, ripples through society, and transforms public life. Deep social change can arise from a single person's thirst for absolute perfection.

His desire for perfection in his work can be explained, in part, by historical circumstance. When Juan Ramón left his native Andalusia in 1900 and made his first trip to Madrid, Spain was recovering from a catastrophe. Two years earlier she had been soundly defeated by the United States and had lost Cuba, Puerto Rico, and the Philippines. That humiliation touched off an intense public debate about her future.

Two issues in that discussion affected the course of Juan Ramón's creative life: the need to re-create both Spanish poetry and the Spanish language, and the role of work in his country's intellectual reconstruction.

He sensed, to begin with, that one could not "remake" one's country without remaking her language, and that the best way to change language is through poetry. A great poet—the one Juan Ramón hoped to become—alters common language and, with it, the thought and feeling of others. Change the way people speak and you will change the way they act. After the 1898 disaster it seemed urgent, to Juan Ramón and others, to set aside the rhetoric of imperial Spain—a Spain that had ceased to exist—and to speak more quietly and intimately. Poetry—the highest, most memorable form of speech—had spent too much time in public places. She seemed full of useless pomp and noise. Juan Ramón wanted to build her a "house of time and silence."

I dreamed for our language a poetry that would be both ideal and material, spiritual and sensual, melodious, lovely, mysterious, enchantingly universal, like the best of ancient Greek, Indian, Chinese, or Arabic poetry, or modern English; with less rhetoric and less nationalism; poetry of an altogether higher order, with more breeze and more freedom. A constant poetry, like the one sought by St. John of the Cross or [Gustavo Adolfo] Bécquer, but more abundant and richer.

In his hands, over the next fifty years, Spanish prose became more supple and suggestive. Spanish poetry lay aside certain habits of declamation, sharpened its five senses, and entered transcendental realms little explored until then. No one since Don Luis de Góngora had lavished such care on his language, and no poet since St. John of the Cross had expressed ecstasy so precisely and so simply.

Allied to this effort to renew language and poetry was Juan Ramón's faith in the power of work to renew both the individual and society. Overwhelmingly, the writers of his generation—from Miguel de Unamuno and José Ortega y Gasset to Antonio Machado and Pío Baroja—portray Spaniards as stricken with *aboulia:* spiritual and physical listlessness. It seemed that, at a moment no one could remember, Spain had lost her will to work. Above all, Juan Ramón thought, she had better learn more respect for intellectual labor and the pursuit of beauty:

O Beauty — poetry, art, science — how are you to live
in my country, without respect and without silence;
live with some of these inferior animals, who peep
through the keyhole to see you going by: sad,
tender, naked . . . !

"If God were, and were a Spaniard," he joked, "it
would take less than a month for people to lose all respect for Him." The work he took upon himself was "to
impose, with all my spirit, all that is refined, delicate,
and exquisite about Spain over whatever is coarse,
ugly, and unpleasant."

Defending his solitude and keeping at bay the noisy
"materialism" of Spain and the world, Juan Ramón
tried to make his life a heroic, radiant example of *el trabajo gustoso:* work embraced willingly, with pleasure and
delight.

"Spain is not going to be made on a street corner or
in a café or in the newspapers," he said; and reflected
that if his country was to rise again proudly from its
"foundation of good granite and myrtle," there must be
a few hundred people working passionately to set the
tone for others.

In his youth, reading Shelley, Juan Ramón had
underlined the famous dictum "Poets are the unac-
knowledged legislators of the world." He would spend
his life attempting to practice a "political poetics," an
"ethical aesthetics": an art without an explicitly political

9

"message" but one with deep and subtle effects upon public sensibility. Every day he felt more certain that social improvement would come not from programs of public reform, not from "those unforgivably amateur actors," the "political phantoms who rule us." It would come, instead, from a small but growing number of individual workers, an "immense minority," each of whom loved his own livelihood and delighted in his own daily work:

> Constant, endless fervor
> of my work.
> Restlessness
> held in a chalice! . . .

> Burning wave, feeling
> and fire, in the goblet
> of a happy will.

Part of his own work lay in teaching, and to younger poets he was a devoted and generous mentor. He prepared the way for them, renewing nearly all the forms of Spanish poetry, from the folk song and ballad to the sonnet and free verse. Alluding to that formal renewal, Robert Bly says of Juan Ramón that he "threw up light and airy houses made out of willows, and in so many different designs that all the coming Spanish poets found themselves living in one or another of his willow houses before they moved out to their own . . ."

An excellent group of poets came to maturity around him: Jorge Guillén, Pedro Salinas, Luis Cernuda, Federico García Lorca, Rafael Alberti, Gerardo Diego, and José Bergamín. Lorca acknowledged him as a "master," and it was partly thanks to Juan Ramón that he could declare proudly in 1935, before the dispersal caused by the Civil War, that Spanish poetry was the finest being written in Europe. Juan Ramón taught them never to hurry; not to court the multitude; and to accept responsibility for all aspects of their work, from its conception to its careful revision and its appearance on the printed page. Above all, he taught them to live their lives for poetry alone, to live poetry as an all-embracing passion in which they could "burn completely" (page 184).

He was, perhaps, too stern a teacher, too implacable a defender of his own vision of poetry (one that valued sentiment more than the lightning flash of metaphor), and it was not long before he was at odds with almost all his young disciples. In a series of pen portraits, he sharpened his prose on their weaknesses until he found himself in nearly total solitude, quoting the Spanish proverb "Bring up ravens, and they will eat out your eyes." "They will eat my eyes," he wrote bitterly, "because my eyes [still] nourish them." It was an ugly struggle, but not a useless one: he did, after all, impart to his disciples his own fierce sense of independence. "The job of a poet," he said, "is not to kill poets by creating disciples," but vice versa.

Struggling with the Page

Like any perfectionist, Juan Ramón was unimaginably difficult to live with, and the tangle of his eccentricities — his *cosas* — sometimes exasperated even his wife, Zenobia Camprubí Aymar, whose cheer, strength, and devotion were legendary. How often she must have smiled ironically, collected her things, and gone off to see friends, or out on business, gently closing the door on his imagined ailments, his hatred of noise, his allergies, his need for "outer order and spiritual restlessness."

One of his peculiarities — to him it was a curse — was that he could not stop writing: poems in verse and in prose, aphorisms, lectures, critical essays, letters, translations of Yeats and Blake, Shakespeare and Shelley, and (with Zenobia) many volumes of the Hindu poet Tagore. His unbelievable abundance as a writer kept him in anguish over the revision, arrangement, and publication of his works. The central drama of his life was this struggle with the page: "the printed page and the empty one!"

He had avid readers . . . but how to place his poems in their hands? How to reach his own "immense minority"? At first he was content to publish books of poems: fifteen of them by 1916, and another seven by 1923.*

Those individual books were revised and transformed, sensibly enough, into volumes of selected verse (his personal *antologías*). But such partial offerings were never able to keep pace with his rhythm as a worker (from one to three poems per day), and over the years he turned despairingly from one solution to another. He brought out several series of exquisite *cuadernos*: pamphlets combining his own work with that of younger poets and artists. Perfect, but too expensive! He resigned himself to seeing his poems and prose in the daily newspapers: worn, ugly typefaces, humiliating misprints, the nasty surprise of sharing space with ads for cough medicine or lice repellent. He thought of finding an obedient printer and paying him to print up his daily work (fifty copies would do!), or of purchasing a printing press and installing it in his basement. These were provisional measures. They arose from his belief that a poet should work and produce continuously, following his own "vegetative rhythm," like "a gentle force of nature." From about 1924 he felt certain that what

---

* Two of the best known were *Platero y yo* (Platero and I), a book of elegiac prose poems about a young man's love for his donkey and for their Andalusian surroundings; and *Diario de un poeta reciencasado* (Diary of a Newly Married Poet), inspired by a sea voyage to the United States, where he married Zenobia.

mattered was his work as a whole: not his "collected poems," not his "works," but his *Work*, his *Obra*, in the singular: the book to end all books and restore the universe to Silence. That work would be all *presence*. He wanted to revise his work entirely into the present, reliving it as he revised, in order to feel again, in a single, eternal moment, every poem he had ever written. Like a god, he would be fully conscious, at once, of his entire creation:

> I would like my book
> to be like the sky at night,
> all present truth, without history.
>
> I want it, like the sky,
> to give itself entirely at each instant,
> with all its stars . . .

His ideas of how to bring that "total" book into material existence changed incessantly over the years. It would form one organic work of poetry and prose, *Metamorphosis*, in twenty-one? fourteen? . . . in *seven* volumes, beginning with a gathering of aphorisms (*Ideolojía*) and ending with the sources of his poems and the efforts of his imitators (among his papers are parts of an anthology, with acerbic comments, entitled *My Best Echo*). It was a project too vast for any one life, and he was often overwhelmed by depression. His daily struggle for wholeness, his longing for completion, caused him to confront his own mortality, and it is not surprising that he devoted so much thought to death (page 131), teaching himself to accept it calmly as an element in the total equation of his work.

In 1936, on the outbreak of the Civil War, Juan Ramón was named Cultural Attaché of the Spanish Embassy in Washington and was separated from his books and papers. In his Madrid apartment he had left the entire "rough draft" of his *Obra*: thousands of pages of poetry, personal correspondence, and notes. And yet in exile his work flowered once again in mystical poems and prose—seven more published books—about the god within him and the immanence of that god in nature. Two of his masterpieces from that period were *Dios deseado y deseante* (God Desired and Desiring) and, in prose, *Españoles de tres mundos* (Spaniards of Three Worlds), a collection of his pen portraits, the best biographical prose ever written by a Spaniard.

An enemy of fascism, he refused to return to Spain, then ruled by Franco, and spent the last twenty years of his life in New York, Havana, Riverdale (Maryland), Coral Gables, and, finally, Puerto Rico, where he received word in 1956 that he had been awarded the Nobel Prize for Literature, for having given the world "an inspiring example of spirituality and artistic purity." The honor meant little to him, for Zenobia died of cancer three days after the announcement. Juan

Ramón was defeated by her death: for forty years she had been his beloved and constant companion, solving the problems of daily life and allowing him to concentrate fully on his poetry. Unable to write anymore, he died himself a year and a half later.

The Quest for Brevity

As early as 1900 he had begun to write aphorisms, and by the time of his death, had accumulated more than four thousand of them. The aphorism seemed to summon perfection and to challenge it: it is both easier and harder to be perfect in a few words than in many. It was also, like the short poem, a sign of reverence for the silence that contains all meaning. Speak exactly and you will speak less, perhaps not at all. So much the better: "Better to be quiet than to speak . . ." (page 56). In his writing Juan Ramón, like Mallarmé, wished to create a perfect universe where writing and speech are unnecessary: "Writing poetry is preparation for unwritten poetry," for silence. To him, the aphorism represented a "concession." It was what you did "in the meantime."

So as not to argue with myself about the conviction, the duty, the need not to write anymore, I write all the time, at every moment. As a friendly concession to the writer in me, I write the aphorism, the short song, the epigram.

Often, he tells us, he grew tired of discursive prose, tired of reading novels and plays that take us on a "more or less lyrical detour," only to lead us back "to the life from which we were trying to escape." He loved brevity and the "surprise of sudden illumination." There were times when he thought the world would be "a more civilized," considerate place if the poet, the philosopher, and the historian went straight to their conclusions. Not that there wasn't room for "stentorian poets of laughter and wailing, but

> who says there can't be a place, also, for quiet, serene ones, for when we need quiet and serenity? Ah, to be one of them! One of the poets whose song helps close the wound rather than open it!

Poetry, Work, and Business

Many of Juan Ramón's aphorisms are about the work of writing. Hard work, to be sure, and many a writer, including Juan Ramón, has compared himself to a manual laborer. Poets use that image to demystify their work (the poem is only a well-made mechanism meant to elicit certain emotions from the reader), or to persuade the world that they are actually *doing* something in their apparent idleness. Or they use it sentimentally, as Neruda does, to turn poetry into a sign of solidarity with those for whom they are writing. But unsentimental Auden, who sometimes used that image himself, raises an important objection. The laborer or craftsman can foresee the product of his labor—he knows more or less what he is trying to do or make—while very often the poet cannot. When he begins a poem, the poet is entering the unknown.

No, the poet's hands are not really those of a manual laborer. And yet, in the words of Sir Philip Sidney, the Renaissance courtier, of all "workmen" the poet is the "most excellent." Poetry and work: there will always be a bond between them, as there is between work and business. But in poetry the bond is much closer than in business. In the work of poetry, work takes off its business clothes and stands before us stark naked.

Poetry helps us see more easily what work is, helps us remember that it is a spiritual impulse which does not always belong to business. The poet helps us remove work from its "institutional" framework, and meditate upon it the way we meditate upon love apart from the social institution of marriage. Seen as poetry, work touches upon everything that matters: it gives our lives rhythm; deepens our appreciation of silence, nature, and dream; brings the present into vivid existence; and consoles us for being mortal.

In this age of the temporary worker, when we are reminded each day of the frailty of our bonds to this or that institution—university, company, union, industry—it is good to hear a poet evoke the part of our work that is entirely spiritual, that is not for sale, and that can strive, impossibly, for perfection. There is comfort in the stoical thought that no social force can prevent anyone from working. A poet symbolizes that proud independence. He can better the world through his work, but how little he requires for it. Not even paper and pencil.

The Leap Toward Poetry

The Complete Perfectionist preaches to the converted—or rather, addresses them quietly. It was written for those who know what it is to dream of perfect writing and perfect work. It is a book of suggestions and hints rather than of instruction or advice. Like any teacher, Juan Ramón liked to give advice, but in his aphorisms he often draws back from doing so: "Let no one take advice from this book; the only thing that matters is one's own experience." Because not everyone *has* much experience, "the only useful advice would be that given by the young to the old." Juan Ramón was, after all, an individualist, intent upon his own perfection, and these pages show him in dialogue more often with himself than with the reader. There are many, many "lessons" about work in this book, but they do not always come to us directly, in the second person. The *you* is often *him,* not us. Juan Ramón wondered whether art can "instruct" at all:

> Art is not actively didactic, no. But it is clear that the perfect fruit of the cultivated spirit—a spirit intent only upon its own perfection—can educate others through example.

How, then, to *apply* these aphorisms to one's own life and work? Each chapter of this book takes up a necessary element of perfect work. But *within* each chapter, the aphorisms—and occasionally, short poems—go off in their own directions, without following a rigid line of reasoning.

Juan Ramón's writing on dream and reverie throws some light on how to read this book. Part of reading lies in rational analysis. But good reading, like good work, means listening to the odd associations that arise from reverie. What is *not* said—what is suggested in the white space between each aphorism—matters as much as the aphorism itself: "Between idea and idea, a dream!" These aphorisms do not need to be taken by force, at one sitting: they can be returned to and read somewhat randomly and dreamily. Juan Ramón did not like the idea of laboring over a poem—or, presumably, an aphorism—to get at its meaning ("Sad flower, forced open!"):

> When I don't understand a poem, or part of it, I don't insist: I try to be satisfied with what I understand, and I'm sure that another time, under other conditions, I'll understand more and understand something else . . . The understanding of a poem comes in successive surprises.

These aphorisms, too, come in "successive surprises." Reading them requires an imaginative *leap,* across all that is not explained, from poetry to other kinds of work. To make that leap, you must get a running start on one side or the other of the empty space: you must either love poetry or love your own work. Auguste Rodin, who was in love with sculpture, describes such a leap in his own reading:

> Whoever understands one thing, understands all, for the same laws are in everything. I have learned sculpture, and have known well that that was something great. I recall that once when I was reading *The Imitation of Christ,* especially in the third book, I replaced the word "God" everywhere with "sculpture," and it worked, and it was right.

Not all of us, thank God, are poets or sculptors. But we must be poets enough to daydream while we read and to avoid receiving this "poetics of work" in too literal a manner. Rodin was right: whatever is written lovingly about *any* work speaks to our own, but only when we love whatever it is that we do.

Here, then, are the words of a great worker: sparks from his anvil. May they help you love the work of poetry, and find something like poetry in your work.

Christopher Maurer
Vanderbilt University
September 1996

Self

Through work we define ourselves, and upon our work we leave our image. It is part of who we are, and who we shall become.

One of Juan Ramón's best-known works in progress was his *I*, his public self. Over the years, in a series of vignettes and aphorisms (like the ones on the following pages), he portrayed himself as god, as nature, as his own disciple and master; in short, as a sufficient, alternate universe.

Like his poetry, that *I*, that public ego, was in a constant state of revision. In his earliest poses for the photographer, one sees the sad, dark eyes of a self-declared "martyr of Beauty," a "precision instrument for thinking and feeling." The well-trimmed beard and careful, elegant attire suggest a master of perfection: "My kingdom lies in the difficult." His look could be sharp and fastidious, and one or two of the photos might have been inscribed with the aphorism "Let us cultivate, be-

fore all else, the art of rejection!" On an imaginary calling card—one of many he handed to posterity—he
engraved the words

THE UNIVERSAL ANDALUSIAN

In one of his autobiographical pen portraits, he catches
his reflection in a windowpane and finds that his head
"bears a stunning resemblance to those of Góngora,
Calderón, and Shakespeare."

Not surprisingly, his enemies called him Narcissus.
They were right, he replied. All gods, and therefore all
poets, fall in love with their own creation; and all male
creators fall in love with the poetic, feminine side of
themselves. But Narcissus, too, was misunderstood.
What he saw in the water was an image not of himself
but of completion and worldly beauty. When he peered
into the pool, into the very "eye of Nature," Narcissus
longed to escape from himself and dissolve into the universe: the noblest sort of metamorphosis. More stinging
than "Narcissus," Juan Ramón thought, were the
names his mother called him as a child: "Juanito the
Demanding, Johnny the Question Mark, Little Mr.
Spoiled, the Interrupter, John-John the Whimster, Mr.
Invention, Madman, the Exaggerator, the Whiner, the
Pest . . . the Prince."

Was it really *him*, that *I*, that column spiraling endlessly around itself? Why did he show it so insistently

in public, in newspapers and poetry magazines, where it was sure to awaken hostility to his poems and lend itself to ridicule? There is no easy answer. He called himself both a Classic and a Romantic. The Romantic project of his life—his *Work*, his *Obra* (page 14)—required a hero; and especially when he was young, the hero needed to be misunderstood, needed to overcome a rude and hostile world. Where no hostility existed, it had to be provoked, or teased into existence. He must have had great fun baiting others with those public "selves," chuckling at those who took them too seriously.

"In me, there are at least three *I*'s," he once wrote. "I was always enough with two of them. But I want to be my third, the demanding one, *el exijente*."* So many Juan Ramóns, each in search of perfection! There is the *I* of some of the autobiographical aphorisms: the proud martyr of Beauty, the Universal Andalusian. There is the ecstatic *I* of the poems, the selfless Narcissus in love with solitude and the beauty of the world. And there is the worker, the humble *me* who wrote the other two into existence: the *exijente* who struggled endlessly to write perfectly. Life in exile brought another sort of self-fragmentation. In the United States and Puerto Rico, Juan Ramón heard himself speak in the tongue of

* The normal spelling is *exigente*, but one of Juan Ramón's eccentricities was to write *j*, and not *g*, before an *i* or an *e*.

another, and heard others speak in a tongue that was, and was not, his own.

Those selves are not easily reconciled and not easily separated. Who can say where one ends and another begins; which is public or which private? Identity is the deepest of human mysteries, and no identity is more mysterious than that of someone whose life is his art. "To live is to create, and re-create, ourselves," he wrote. No final solution is possible, no identity definitive. It would be harder to imagine an artist of greater integrity. But the notion of identity—of remaining "the very same" person—was alien to him. Here, as everywhere in his thought, perfection lies in succession, transition, metamorphosis:

> To poetize is to become a new *I* each day in a new vision and expression of myself and of the world that I see, my world . . . This passing of the torch from one *I* to another, and from me to the person who follows me, these stages in a beautiful career of light, are the way I conceive of life.

Juan Ramón loved the idea of life as an orbit: "We are nothing but wanderers in orbit. We can never reach an end, never reach ourselves, unless the end is, simply, to run after ourselves."

One of the final names he gave himself was El Cansado de su Nombre (Tired of his Name). We can imagine that, in life and in art, Juan Ramón grew tired of himself and of his names; tired, even, of his pronouns.

> I am not I.
> > I am this one
> Walking beside me whom I do not see.
> Whom at times I manage to visit,
> And at other times I forget.
> The one who remains silent when I talk,
> The one who forgives, sweet, when I hate,
> The one who takes a walk when I am indoors,
> The one who will remain standing when I die.

> (Translated by Robert Bly)
> C.M.

Nature has given me two irreconcilable virtues: supreme productivity and the yearning for supreme perfection . . . Thus my martyrdom—for Beauty—and my melancholy.

What a struggle within me between the complete and the perfect!

What a great thing it is: to be absolute master of perfection and scorn it like this!

I have Poetry hidden in my house, for her pleasure and mine. And the two of us behave like lovers.

I would give the better half of my work not to have written the other.

My best work is my constant repentance for my work.

I am eternal. I have no possible solution.

I am so abstracted in the eternal that spiders have woven cobwebs between my feet.

I want to be, at the same time, the arrow and the spot where it penetrates, or gets lost.

I like not the event but its representation. For in the event I am only a participant or a spectator, and in the representation of it I am a creator, a poet.

They ask me, "Why don't you do this thing or that?"
   I answer, "Because what I live on is precisely not doing them. I live negating their affirmation or affirming their negation."

They say I am monotonous. True. All I sing is the universe.

My only two weapons: time and silence.

My life never has a beautiful present. The best of it lies in memory and in hope.

My life is constant regret for not having done things I refused to do when I could have.

In order to disorder my inner life, I have to tidy up my outer one.

I don't smoke, don't drink wine, hate coffee and bull-fighting, religion and militarism, the accordion and the death penalty. I live only for, and by, Beauty . . .

My work is—they say—unreal. Unreal, yes. But quiet and eternal amid the madness of life, like the shadow of a castle in the water that tries to carry it away.

Some of my affectionate envious friends say, "You write too much."

"Maybe," I answer. "But as long as the best of your little is worse than the worst of my much, I will keep on doing so."

I believe in the "great poet," who isn't the one who reaches the widest public but the one who creates the most public.

Even greater would be the poet who could build the total, immense minority.

That is my own illusion.

"Glory" (what a word!) consists in going from the *me* that others don't know to the other *me* that I don't know.

It is frightful to have a double in life. In poetry, doubly frightful.

But it calms us when a third person takes our double to be a single.

The Universal Andalusian.

Tired of his Name.

In the End

Hidden creator of an unapplauded star.

Rhythm

The two most basic elements of work are time and rhythm. Unless we have the freedom to master these two elements, and use them wisely, there can be no happiness in work and no perfection, only the monotony of alienated labor. There is another, related element which work has in common with music and to which Juan Ramón devoted much thought, tempo: the deliberate quickness or slowness of what we are doing. His advice, always, is to go slowly: "Don't try to race ahead of the hours." Again and again he returns to this paradoxical formula: "Slowly, you will do everything quickly."

For Juan Ramón, perfect work depends upon a vivid sense of wholeness. A year, season, month, day, and hour of work are complete in themselves, but they are felt as part of something larger. "I do not divide up my life into days but my days into lives; each day, each hour [is] an entire life," to be used as fully as possible.

His need to imagine his life's work as an entirety made him compare each period of it to a "movement" in a symphony. It is an ambitious analogy, but a good one, for work—like poetry and music—endows time with rhythm. In fact, rhythm is *the meaning we give to time*, and therefore the right rhythm of work gives meaning and wholeness to our workday and to our lives.

The freedom to endow work with rhythm (and therefore meaning) is denied to most of the world's workers. Those working *against* time to meet a sales or production quota cannot hope to find the sort of working rhythm to which Juan Ramón is referring. To find that rhythm, one must dwell comfortably within the hour, as within one's own house or body. For many, the hour is a rented room, the landlord is implacable, and the rent—the quota—falls due with sickening frequency.

In 1934–35, as Juan Ramón worked incessantly both on his poetry and on his "poetics of work," the French philosopher Simone Weil had obtained a year's leave from the lycée at which she was teaching, and taken a job in a factory in order to experience firsthand the plight of France's industrial workers. What she noticed about time and rhythm conforms exactly to the thought of Juan Ramón and poses a challenge to all employers. "Time and rhythm constitute the most important factor of the whole problem of work," she wrote. "[Our] thought was intended to master time, and this vocation . . . must be kept inviolate in every man." Weil was observing assembly-line workers called upon "to execute at high speed, in a specified order, five or six simple movements, indefinitely repeated, each lasting a second or thereabouts." The wise lessons she drew from all this are as applicable to intellectual work—to writing or designing or the management of resources—as they are to factory labor.

The succession of their movements is not designated in factory parlance by the word "rhythm," but by "cadence." This is only right, for that succession is the contrary of rhythm. Any series of movements that participates of the beautiful and is accomplished with no loss of dignity implies moments of pause, as short-lived as lightning flashes, but that are the very stuff of rhythm and give the beholder, even across extremes of rapidity, the impression of leisureliness. The foot racer, at the moment of beating the world's record, seems to glide home slowly while one watches his inferior rivals making haste behind him. The better and more swiftly a peasant swings his scythe the more the onlookers have the impression that, as the invariable phrase goes, he is taking his time. On the other hand, the spectacle presented by men over machines is nearly always one of wretched haste destitute of all grace and dignity. It comes naturally to a man, and it befits him, to pause on having finished something, if only for an instant, in order to contemplate his handiwork, as God did in Genesis. Those lightning moments of thought, of immobility and equilibrium, one has to learn to eliminate utterly in a working day at the factory.

No doubt conditions have improved in the factories in which Weil worked. But her distinction between "rhythm" and metronomic "cadence" remains, in most of the world, as vivid as it was in the 1930s. That momentary "pause on having finished something," the pause that distinguishes workers from animate tools, is the moment Juan Ramón refers to as "revision," and the ideal rhythm of which Simone Weil wrote resembles the one he pursued in his own daily work. His thoughts on rhythm remind us that the control of time, and the possibility of rhythm, must be granted to the worker, to the extent possible, if work is to possess any meaning at all. Alienated workers everywhere tell the same story. Their time is broken down, fragmented, not their own.

Like all perfectionists, Juan Ramón worried that his own internal rhythm—his "ideal day" as a worker—did not often correspond to the hours of the clock: "I cannot divide the day into twenty-four hours or twelve. My days sometimes have half an hour, and others three, and others a thousand." He is absorbed in the *present* of his work, and clock time passes him by unnoticed, or breaks into his thought like an unwanted noise or guest. He longs for total concentration in all that he does (see "Silence" and "The Present"), and to reach that inner stillness, there can be no urgency to "finish" something, no regret for yesterday's failures, no "nostalgia for the past pleasurable hours," only new hours of pleasure in the present. Intent upon his work, he begins each morning with his own version of "one day at a time": "One of my morning prayers: 'Keep things from sticking to me, dawn! Let this day be only today!'" A day, he thought, should be only a day, like an island "in the sea of time, between its morning and its night." He dreamt of making "each hour an hour: a round, smooth, well-defined thing which does not go poking into the hour beside it." And yet, when the days or hours are placed beside one another, they ought to bear fruit or procreate "like male and female in heat."

He struggled endlessly against his own desire to be done in a hurry and against his longing to be working on something else, and inscribed on the title page of some of his books a thought from Goethe: "Like a star, without haste, but without rest, let man revolve around his work." He tried to combine into a single rhythm his days of creation and his days of revision or idleness. Here, as in all he did, he drew inspiration from the slow, successive rhythms of the tides and the seasons. He dreamed that, thanks to his faithful daily rhythm, he would leave the world having spent all of himself on his work, having "emptied" himself into it. He smiled to think that, when worn out by work, there would be nothing of him for death to claim: "Day after day, I have been putting my whole life into my work. Death? 'I' will not be buried. Only my shell will go down to the earth." What of the "pause" spoken of by Simone Weil? Here is the way he imagined such a pause, on the last day of his life, in the confidence that his work had been completed:

That day, that day
when I look at the sea—the two of us calm—
trusting in it; all my soul
emptied fully into my Work—
forever certain, like a great tree
on the coast of the world,
with its certain leaves and certain roots,
and the great work that is finished!

That day, on which
to sail will be to rest, when I have worked
on me so much, so much, so much!
That day, that day
when death—black waves—no longer courts me,
and I smile endlessly on everything,
knowing I leave so little

—just the bare bones—
so very little of myself.

C.M.

Work, solitude, time.

All the work of the universe is no more than time and rhythm, rhythm and time. Balance, and a means to make that balance.

Of all the rhythms of the world, the most harmonious is—can be—that of our own life.

Whoever finds it is happy in body and soul and gives that happiness to others.

My "apartness," my "resonant solitude," the "golden silence" that others have always reproached me for, and have placed beside me in a supposed "ivory tower" that I always saw in a corner of my house and never used . . . I didn't learn them from some false sense of aristocracy, but from the only true aristocracy.

I learned them as a child, in Moguer, from the field-hand, the carpenter, the knife sharpener, the saddlemaker, the mason, and the sailor who worked, alone, on their estate, their workshop or ship, with body in soul, and above all on Sundays, out of truth and faith and joy in their slow, daily pleasurable work.

Let man revolve around his work like a star, without haste but without rest.

A slow haste.

Go slowly in art: let each hour give us what it should. Don't try to race ahead of the hours.

What a pleasure to isolate the day! Like a life in the sea of time, between its morning and its night!

And the hour. If someone could teach me to isolate the hour!

How to give the same dimensions to every hour into which we distribute the day?

How can we make an hour an hour: a round, smooth, well-defined thing that does not go poking into the hour beside it?

In my day, the neighboring hours are like male and female in heat.

When you feel hurried, walk more slowly.

Slowly, you will do everything quickly.

Spring returns more rapidly each year. How will I keep time with the rose?

To work isn't to do a lot in a hurry or, above all, many times; it is to make unique, very well made things.

Doing things badly does not give you the right to demand haste from the person who does things well.

Let's not force things, but let everything arrive at its own moment, in its own peculiar manner, fusing its rhythms with ours.

My books have never run after fame; each of them has arisen in its own place at its own hour.

What a struggle between my two rhythms, the whimsical and the normal. Which should conquer, which conquer itself?

Work, like life, is resolved successively.

When you leave one thing for another, change rhythm. And be careful with those runaway rhythms that send us wheeling downhill!

Every day I draw up a plan, and by the next day I have abandoned it. My soul is tattooed with useless inscriptions.

"Lost" days, so full of finds!

In the life of the intellect, one should have, from time to time, a day of synthesis, analyzing and polishing the labor of days past: something like the beginning of a new life.

We ought to learn the marvelous rhythm of "meanwhile . . ."

Sometimes I think I'm caressing an idea, and I am caressing a rhythm.

When an extraneous rhythm—or lack of rhythm—steals away that of my work, I have to recover it, tapping my foot on my head!

To work, to work even at night, so my eyes will be worn out when they go back to the earth!

Silence

Good work arises from silence: not necessarily from noiselessness but from the fervent concentration of which silence is an image. For obviously, inner silence can occur in the midst of noise. Silence is oneness and wholeness. For Juan Ramón, noise leads to dispersion: it "shatters my day and my brain into a thousand irreparable little pieces."

Silence is deafness to distraction, to "noise in the head": the sting of yesterday's insult, plans for the future. It is deafness to all that makes it impossible to hear and follow the rhythm of our work. And in fact, in a subtle way, some work, like some music or poetry—Juan Ramón's, for example—sharpens our awareness of silence. The poem, the sonata, or the well-made object seems to deepen silence or hallow it or reorder it, making it almost palpable. Silence shimmers with form.

Not only Juan Ramón's own poetry but his comments about the work of others show that he was unusually sensitive to the *sound* of poems. For example, when he speaks about the noises he loves, he evokes "the verses of a poet, which hardly make any sound along the edge, with all the sound at the center" (page 59). He is alluding to his love of assonance: the gentle sound of vowels rather than the chime of both vowels and consonants. He is remembering how Cordelia, in *King Lear*, scorns the hollow eloquence of her sisters and wishes only to "love, and be silent." As a poet, he thought often about her apology for silence and simplicity:

> Nor are those empty-hearted whose low sounds
> Reverb no hollowness.

In his later years, when he was living in exile, he transcribed hundreds of pages of his verse into prose, "with all the sound at the center" rather than at the end of each line. That is the way his poems sometimes appear in posthumous editions. "The word," he wrote, "was made for the ear, not the eye." And he told a friend, pressing the point after a recital he had given for some blind children in Puerto Rico, "Take a poem and recite it, and pretend that your listeners are blind."

To hear the sound of his poems and those of others and the counterpoint of his own thought, he needed more silence than Madrid or his own fortitude could provide. The noises around him, the loudspeakers of movie houses, the cries of street vendors, the seventy-year-old woman—the landlady herself!—learning to sing in the apartment beneath him, made him think bitterly about society's scorn for intellectual labor. "My effort to reach ethical and aesthetical perfection is enormous; but the effort of everyone else to prevent that from happening is infinitely greater." He was engaged, he thought, in giving Spain her first "universal poet." Why couldn't Spain keep quiet?

There was nothing he could do about the noisy flock of sparrows under his window (in one apartment, he looked down onto the trees in the courtyard of a sanatorium where he had lived years earlier). But what of the *people* around him? He spoke with envy of a certain legendary cork-lined room—France had allowed Proust to ennoble *her* with his work!—and he consulted with some carpenters. His faithful chronicler, Juan Guerrero Ruiz, reports that they insulated one wall of Juan Ramón's workroom with "a cushion made from sacking and esparto grass." A day or two later, the poet complained that the noises were coming through as clear as ever, at least in *his* direction; "for all I know, the neighbor's apartment is much quieter." When the noise became unbearable, he and Zenobia packed up and moved. They did so every few years. "All of our moves have been to flee from noise," Juan Ramón told Guerrero. "We left our apartment on Conde de Aranda because some Cuban ladies were playing the piano and dancing in the apartment upstairs . . ." In that apartment there had also been problems with a cricket. Two or three crickets, actually (page 55). On the balcony of the apartment next door, a few feet from Juan Ramón's worktable, a little boy and his sister had hung a cricket cage. Juan Ramón complained politely—in his beautiful, nearly illegible script—to their father, an architect, the Count of Manila. The count answered in a poem. He could understand very little of Juan Ramón's "indecipherable logoglyphics," but had made out the word *grillo.* He was pleased to inform him that the latter had escaped that very night from its tiny prison. Unaware of political correctness, Juan Ramón consoled the girl with a doll, and the boy with some books, and the count sent the poet and Zenobia a basket of red carnations.

"And we moved from our apartment at Lista, 8 because one of our neighbors made our lives impossible," he continues. "Velázquez, 96 was ruined when they brought together two trolley lines under our window." For Juan Ramón, each move meant packing up thousands of pages of work in progress and falling further behind in his revision.

Outer silence—noiselessness—was nowhere to be found. Very well, then, he would simply build up his inner resistance. Unable to have silence, he persuaded himself that he needed at least a little noise. "Better than the deserted, absolute backwaters of silence, a warning fence of distant and diffuse human noise." We *need* noise in order to create, he told himself. In fact, where it doesn't exist "we will 'make' it," or imagine it. "Without noise I go swimming, flying, jumping over things; with noise, limping and bumping and stumbling into them. But both possibilities are good . . ."

C.M.

The Real Cricket

What anguish, that single cricket from that singularly strange month of June (concave, deep June!), right there above my open window, nibbling into my solitude like a harness bell in the inner center of my inner ear! My reverie darkened into an infinite nightmare, into the whole black sky of summer: into the monotonous pounding of raindrops; leaden stars in an eternity of shadow; immense ocean of black shoe polish rippling into one brief and terrible wave that left me choking and gasping for air at each rhythmic blow. The entire world in concentration, bearing down on my auditory brain, holding me and yanking me by the head . . . until I could stand it no longer, and asked Honorito Igelmo, the concierge's son, master of the real cricket, if he would sell it to me. I told him I would give him five pesetas or ten or twenty-five, or whatever he wanted, with the idea of carrying the steely, dark little animal to the park and finding a new home for it, far away, in some grassy spot.

The little boy stared at me with enormous eyes that reminded me of two big melancholy, deeply and sadly singing crickets, and I wondered if my question had caused him pain.

No, it had not. There *was* a god of silence and he was watching over me that day.

"For twenty-five pesetas," said the little Castilian, "I'll bring the gentleman five of the best crickets he can imagine!"

Space, time, solitude, silence.

You find in solitude only what you take to it.

Be in your solitude like the water in a garden in the solitude of a Sunday afternoon.

Better to be quiet than to speak; to dream than to be quiet; to read than to dream or think. When we read, silence itself grows quiet, and we can think or dream in company.

"Silence is golden, silence is gold." Silence makes everything fit. It is the great ring of gold.

Unity is the noble daughter of silence; dispersion, the mad stepchild of noise.

Noise shatters my day and brain into a thousand irreparable little pieces.

In silence I can have suspended—suspended in the instant—my entire day and even my entire life, in full synthesis. In noise I can only suspend the instant.

There are days when life becomes concave. How things resound in her—the yapping of dogs, the barking of orders, the screams of children, the chirping of birds, the sighs of women.

Other days it becomes convex, and nothing resounds at all. Or better, everything ceases to sound. And then, how terrifyingly deaf my life is!

How will the deaf man see the sunset?

Silence does not waste time, it fills it. Yes. And the only thing that fills time is silence. So that time shared with noise is time lost. But silence conquers time, puts it back together, and makes it whole.

. . . True music is the music of silence, the silent but well-heard music of thought in the head, passion in the body, reverie in the soul.

Poetry

Listen to the song of the cricket. First ingenuous, vacillating; later, rhetorical and easy; still later, at midnight, pure, contained, serene, intense, forgetting what it is and what it sings with and where it is; like a star; like a star in the water.

Noise: multiple thorn defending who knows what eternal, virgin rose, immense and invisible.

Who—or What—is it that is using noise to defend itself from analysis?

How immortal you are, noise!

Noise, how it complicates everything. What a bothersome guest, so sloppy, so tangible, so dirty, such a fool.

Noise places words in my path like boulders. But somewhere out there, existent and evident, is the level para-
dise, the prairie of silence.

O noises that do nothing to disturb the silence! Noises
like thoughts, like meditations, like a huge force of inner
concentration, when they seem to be listening to themselves, cloaked in their abstraction, in faded outline!
Noises like the verses of a poet, which hardly make any
sound along the edge, with all the sound at the center;
welcome, pleasant noises that I need and love: slow toll-
ing of a bell, wandering little bird, falling beads of
water.

Hearing silence and seeing shadow, our life is more luminous and expressive and dwells more within the eternal — I mean, within the sufficient.

In noise, let us search for what can be done with noise.

When it is noisy, don't sing: draw or sculpt your
thought.

When a noise breaks into your silence, make it immedi-
ately a natural part of your silence.

In our successive search for creative silence, we always find new noise, successive noise. (And when there is none, we will desire it and look for it. We will "make" it, so as to struggle with it . . . and master it?)

What wasted silences there are in life!

The Present

I t barely exists, it pauses for no one, but it is *there* that we must work! In order to do good work, we must defeat what Juan Ramón calls *nostalgia* — the vague longing to be somewhere else in time — and hold to the present. And the present is hard to seize. When we reach for it, our problems pull us away elsewhere, into the past or the future. Work is a way to ripen the hours, to make them heavier. Through work we invite the present to endure. Hold the present with your work, and your work will be present forever.

"Almost all that we can be said to enjoy," wrote Samuel Johnson, "is past or future; the present is in perpetual motion, leaves us as soon as it arrives, ceases to be present before its presence is well perceived, and is only known to have existed by the effects which it leaves behind." Juan Ramón makes it a matter of grammar:

> We have been, we will be.
> Yes. But we never are!

He yearns, always, for perfect—for godlike!—concentration. He wants to *be,* thanks to his work. He wants to be present to his work and in his work, and wants to have all of his work fully present before him (see "Revision"). Noise, remorse, worries about his health, distract him from what he is making. Among his aphorisms are stratagems and prayers for creating a quiet place in time where he can work.

C.M.

Care for this day! This day is life, the very essence of life. In its weightless passage are all the reality and variety of your existence: the pleasure of growing, the glory of action, and the splendor of beauty.

Yesterday is only a dream and tomorrow only a vision. But this day, well used, makes each yesterday a dream of happiness and each tomorrow a vision of hope. So care for this day!

(from the Sanskrit)

To conquer each day with the ideas of each day.

If we do not work drunkenly on our work, we grow bored by time and space: the personified, named external witness of our ennui. When we do grow drunk on our work, time and space are our inner allies, our invisible and anonymous true friends.

There have never been two days, two hours, two minutes, two seconds in which nature, life, or we ourselves have been, are, will be the same, one and the same. So how be bored?

Society and mankind are only and always succession, provisionality, becoming, the present. This is man's great strength: to be always present and to know that he can always be so, whenever he feels that strength within him . . .

Past, Present, Future

The future contains nothing more than the past, it *was* the past. So let us calm down and be happy with our daily present, and hold on to it as long as we can.

Let us grow accustomed to seeing in the present all of the past and all of the future.

How the past clings to the feet of the present so as not to let it reach the future without it!

To console ourselves for this constant nostalgia of the future and the past, let us remember that we are the past of those who will come after us, and the future of those who went before; and besides, we are our own present.

Each day let us sweep away what has passed in order to form a past; that way we will give the life we have left—though it be only an hour—the breadth of all eternity.

When you're working on one thing and start to yearn for another, imagine that the thing you're working on would be the one you would be yearning for if you were working on the other.

Treat the least significant things you do as though they were permanent, and they will endure.

At each instant, to do the best one can. That is enough.

The good has "only" two instants: *its* instant and, a while later, *its* eternity.

Eternity is nothing more than the present. Who "has" the present has eternity.

To embrace all of your work, work much on a little each day.

Your strength: why do you have it if not to spend it? Spend all of it each day. Keep nothing. Each dawn, each day, will give you enough of it. Your strength of tomorrow will add nothing to your strength of today. Your old strength . . . will be nothing but your tradition, your bonds, your sadness . . . Strength of yesterday withheld yesterday: lost! Strength of today given today: won!

Light

Why this scent of flesh and of the infinite in the calm evening? From what radiant woman does it come to me, like a memory of my future life?

> I awoke under the sky,
> poor sunken roof,
> black and red from night and dawn
> with cobwebs, embers, and animals.

Getting up, I arranged it as best I could
and under its faint, ragged blue tent
went slowly to what was mine.
And I called that arrangement my day.

Memory

For Juan Ramón, one of the secrets of finding happiness both in work and in life lay in striking the right balance between remembering and forgetting. "On the scales of your life," give as much to one as to the other. "Watch for their point of equilibrium."

Work, technique, our entire moral self, depend upon remembered experience in more ways than any philosopher or psychologist can enumerate. And yet it annoyed our poet, who longed to live and work within the present, that people think of memory as active, beneficial, and unifying, and of forgetting as memory's passive, lazy "sister."

To *re*member is to put back together into a unified whole, and to forget seems an involuntary coming apart, a dispersion. But both in life and in creative work, it seems clear that an overactive memory can be a hindrance. It was for Juan Ramón: "My ideal would be 'to forget and to make.' But I remember and remember and remember, and do not make."

When the "useless past" distracts us from the work at hand, memories become—in his words—"the seven plagues of the indolent person." And when we dwell too much in the past, or on the work we have done in the past, we lose the uniqueness of the present. The person good at forgetting is strongest not only because he can forgive himself and others but because more of his working moments seem unprecedented and he is better able to concentrate on the work and the beauty that are before him: "Let us respect forgetting, the marvels of forgetting, which allow us to contemplate, isolated from all else, the uniqueness of the present."

Then, too, a memory sometimes needs to vanish completely in order to reveal all of its poetry.

> O secret memories
> far from the paths
> of other ones!

> Memories that, one night,
> rise up suddenly
> like a rose in the desert,
> like a star at noon
> (passion of cold forgetting),
> milestones

of our best life,
the one we can barely live!

How dry
our daily path,
and suddenly
it is Spring. Marvel
of forgotten memories!

When we forget, something new is received into the unconscious and held for later, for "forgetting loses nothing." She does not simply hold our treasure, but transforms it. How often has forgetfulness stolen away the page we were working on and purged it of all that was not . . . memorable. Juan Ramón is right: "To forget is to be reborn."

C.M.

On the scales of your life, give as much to forgetting as to remembering. Watch for their point of equilibrium.

We are constantly worrying, to the point of desperation, about not being able to remember something.

But whether or not we remember it doesn't really matter. We will forget all that we remember and all that we don't.

The balance in our lives comes from making peace between remembering and forgetting. We should not try to force that peace, but let the two of them work it out for themselves, without our intervention.

(Yes, I tell myself, but that isn't really what happens. The fact *is* that we behave like traitors and want to overthrow forgetting—that poor, truthful king—by giving a moment's help to memory.)

Many mistakenly think of memory as an activity, but not forgetting, as though the latter were not also a reality.

Memory doesn't come from a higher power than forgetting.

Forgetting is almost natural; memory, almost artificial.

We oughtn't to forget that earth, air, and water are stronger at forgetting than remembering.

Memory is the daughter of noise; forgetting, the child of silence.

Forgetting is a virtue; memory, a vice.

Memories are the seven plagues of the indolent person.

What could we do to make memory occupy as little time as space?

Poet: to restrain memory is to conquer. To give in to it is to be conquered.

The strongest man: isn't he the one who forgets the most?

Not to relive with pain even a single hour of the past.

For remorse, there is no consolation.

Let us respect forgetting, the marvels of forgetting, which allow us to contemplate, isolated from all else, the uniqueness of the present.

Memory

How sad to carry the treasure of each day (up and down) across the bridge of night (down and up) to the other sun! If only we were content to leave its mantle in the hands of the past; to look no more at what was; to come face to face, pleasurably naked, with the freedom and joy of the present!

> O time, give me the secret
> that makes you newer
> the older you grow!

> Day after day, your past
> is less, and your future greater,
> and your present
> like the instant
> of an almond tree in bloom.

> O time, who leave no tracks,
> tell me how, each day,
> your spirit invades your body.

A good system for beguiling the past—the useless past—is to tell it, "Tomorrow I will remember you . . ." And that way it will wither away without our killing it cruelly, and its memories will not be strong enough to keep pace with our hopes, and will lie behind us, dead in the road.

In the poetic imagination, as in the sea, there may be zones of oblivion, but nothing is ever lost.

Forgetting loses nothing; it stores everything up like treasure. And if we are worthy of memory, she will give us her key to forgetting.

Forgetting contains memory, as nothing contains everything: not in negation or enmity but in unity and affirmation.

. . . Lovely memory, constant worker, generous lover of forgetfulness!

To forget is to be reborn.

Idealism

Near the title page of some of his books, Juan Ramón drew a sprig of parsley. He wanted to remind himself and his readers that *el trabajo gustoso*, pleasurable work, is not necessarily for gain. In ancient Greece, in the Nemean Games, as in the ones at Olympia, athletes competed not for bronze, silver, or gold but for a crown of wild celery—Juan Ramón thought it was parsley—or wild olive.

That sprig of parsley was an emblem of his idealism. Juan Ramón was an idealist in at least two senses of the word.

First, he believed that the poet must capture things in their ideal, perfect form rather than the way they exist in reality. He thought that humanity had become too fond of realism, warning that "life and death are not what we read about in the newspapers."

And second, he thought of work—his own work, all work—as a spiritual pursuit rather than a materialistic one.

According to him, the poet's job is to create an ideal world. This is an ancient idea, expressed by Aristotle and passionately defended by Renaissance writers like Sir Philip Sidney and Francis Bacon.

Juan Ramón believed, like Sidney, that poetry must draw us "to as high a perfection as our degenerate souls, made worse by their clayey lodgings, can be capable of." What does this mean? Simply that the world, as it exists, is imperfect and cannot satisfy our innate craving for perfection, and that we need the poet to give us a taste of something better.

Bacon believed something very similar: the use of poetry is "to give some shadow of satisfaction to the mind of man in those points wherein the nature of things doth deny it." The world is inferior to the soul, and therefore we want "a more ample greatness, a more exact goodness, and a more absolute variety than can be found in the nature of things."

Poet and ideal worker see beyond what *is*, beyond what Juan Ramón dismissed as "useless reality." The poet describes not how things are—for that would be the job of the historian or doctor, natural scientist or lawyer, who try to describe reality and are "captived to the truth of a foolish world." We are given a "brazen" world—one made of brass. Only the poet, ranging freely "within the zodiac of his own wit," gives us a golden one. The poet's making is really a "remaking," a deeply original kind of imitation that draws out the best in all that lies before him. He departs from flawed, unsatisfying particulars and comes as close as possible to a vision of earthly perfection. A poet invents ideal love or boredom, the ideal peach, and even, as Juan Ramón does in this book, ideal work.

It is this habit of seeing beyond reality into the ideal—into what Juan Ramón liked to call "invisible reality"—that the poet shares with anyone who questions "the way things are" and tries to do perfect work. It is this pursuit of the ideal which makes the poet an inspiration to all who work, which makes him, in the words of Sidney, "in the most excellent work . . . the most excellent workman."

As for the other dimension of idealism, Juan Ramón often spoke of a gardener from Seville who drew his happiness, and his only wages, from the poetry of work . . .

C.M.

The Sevillian Gardener

In Seville, in the neighborhood of Triana, in a lovely garden overlooking the Guadalquivir, on a street—it seems almost too much, but it's true—a street named Nightingale . . . From his patio, you could see the sun setting against the cathedral and its tower: fiery rose in the lush dark green. The gardener, a large, refined fellow, used to sell plants and flowers that he cared for, exquisitely, on his balcony. For him, each of his plants was like a woman or a delicate child; together, they were a family of leaves and blossoms. How hard for him to sell them, to let them go, to part with a single one! And this particular spiritual struggle (for he had one every day) was over a pot of hydrangeas.

Some people came to buy it, and after mulling it over and conquering his doubts, he worked out an agreement. He would sell that pot on one condition: he would also take care of it. Away they went with his hydrangea. For a few days the gardener went to see it at the home of its new owners. He would take off the dead leaves, water it, add or remove a bit of soil, and prop it up better against its little trellis. And before he left he would give instructions: "The way you water it is important . . . When it's in the sun, put it like this . . . Be especially careful when it's damp at night . . ." And so forth.

The owners were growing tired of his visits ("All right, all right, you've made your point. We'll see you *next month* . . ."), and the gardener visited them less often; or, rather, he went as often but didn't go inside. He would go down the street and gaze at the hydrangea through the grating of the patio. Or he would enter rapidly, a little embarrassed, on some pretext or other: "I've found this syringe, and it will help you water it better," or "I had forgotten about this little wire," and so on. All this in order to see "his" hydrangea.

And finally one day he appeared, renewed and resolute: "If you don't want me to come take care of it, you can tell me how much you want for it, and I'll take it home with me this very moment." Into his arms he took the big blue flowerpot with the pink hydrangea and, as though it were a girl, carried it away.

The great tree of truth has its roots in the earth and its fruits in the sky.

Since the fruits are ours, how we miss them!

Could anything be more pleasant than to restore to the realm of the idea what reality has already degraded for us?

To the idealists who build sculpture gardens: the ideal cannot exist as a block of stone. It can exist only as an "ever-transparent, ever-moving pillar of flame that goes before us . . ."

For me, the impossible is like the star hidden in the day, and it exists like the sure star of night.

What is glimpsed is more visible and lasts longer than what is seen.

The art of appearances is lovelier than the art of realities.

There are no better draftsmen than dust and shadow.

I would like to peer over the edge of the horizon. There, down deep, waiting for me to fall—to my death?—is what I am yearning for.

Why shouldn't I love, adore, feel reverence for my work if it is the most enduring and loveliest body that I can possibly make for my soul?

[Poetry]

I see her everywhere, I understand her, but she doesn't reveal herself to me. Perhaps it is simply that I cannot find her name.

A poet is merely a discontented person who transforms the world according to his whim—who changes for himself and others the appearance of the creation.

Poetry is like a bird that comes in a moment of rapture from the heavens into our hearts. What takes skill is knowing how to send it from our hearts back into the heavens.

Food, drink, conversation, sex, anything that can be realized and completely enjoyed in the act: none of this is for poetry. Poetry is for whatever cannot be *had;* this is its particular charm.

Poetry is all beauty that cannot be explained and needs no explanation.

In poetry what can be resolved in a circle is never everything. By contrast, what remains half resolved, on a difficult middle ground, is always a path.

Poetry, a substance that nourishes like an essence.

Poetry that doesn't take hold, that isn't contagious, no matter how good it is, is useless.

Poetry is further from the seeker than god* from the mystic or truth from the philosopher. The true seeker of poetry is always less contented with his find than the mystic or the philosopher are with his . . .

Yes, poetry is practical. And the poet is much more useful than the religious person, for what the poet tries to do is create here and now, free to everyone, what the other tries to encounter there and later, and only if we deserve it.

Let us propose a distant goal, far away in an infinite future, and walk toward it each day, slowly, without stopping, enjoying in all their fullness what lies beside the road and what we leave behind.

* "I write god with a small letter the way I write father and mother, glory and sea, earth, sky, etc. And woman. It is not irreverence, but neither is it reverence. It is not fear; it is with a small letter, 'love.' " — JRJ

Nature

The poet calls himself a "maker." From earliest times, he has compared his powers of "making" not only to those of nature but also, without blushing, to those of the divinity, the "Maker of that maker." Sir Philip Sidney presses the point in his lovely *Apology for Poetry*. Surely, he writes, it is "not too saucy a comparison" to "balance the highest point of man's wit with the efficacy of nature." In so doing, the poet

> give[s] right honor to the heavenly Maker of that maker, who having made man to His own likeness, set him beyond and over all the works of that second nature, [for] our erected wit maketh us know what perfection is, and yet our infected will keepeth us from reaching unto it.

For the poet—Sidney, Emerson, Rilke, Keats—the book of nature is (in Juan Ramón's words) "an inexhaustible source of spiritual norms." Nature tells him what and when and how to make. It gives him norms that bear upon his way of life and manner of work and serve as imaginary touchstones for the verbal objects he creates. Emerson tells us of the poet's intuition that

> [his] poems are a corrupt version of some text in nature, with which they ought to be made to tally. A rhyme in one of our sonnets should not be less pleasing than the iterated nodes of a sea-shell, or the resembling difference of a group of flowers. The pairing of the birds is an idyll, not tedious as our idylls are; a tempest is a rough ode, without falsehood or rant . . . Why should not the symmetry and truth that modulate these, glide into our spirits, and we participate the invention of nature?

Juan Ramón is more succinct:

> No matter how short, a line of verse is always longer than a seed; no matter how long, shorter than the tail of a mouse.

To compare human work to the quiet, rhythmic, and endless work of nature, from the growth of a tree to the formation of a seashell or star, is another way to meditate upon perfection. How, Juan Ramón wondered, does one follow nature toward perfection?

If we look at a star, it seems perfect at each moment:
an enchanting, mysterious star. But it is successive,
it is always making itself, always traveling toward
itself, toward its possibility or impossibility . . .

This is one of the "spiritual norms" he derived from
nature. It was that idea of "successiveness," of beauty
in progress, that consoled Juan Ramón for the imperfec-
tions in his own work. He taught himself to think of his
work as a star, a desert, the sea, the sky: images of constant change. Nature, too, is always revising, always
correcting itself and preparing a new version. And as it
does so, nature can suggest the right pace and the right
aesthetic qualities—firmness or delicacy, speed or slowness—for our work. Out walking, in the cool morning,

Rodin plucks a mushroom, delighted, and shows it
to Madame Rodin . . . "Look," he says excitedly,
"and that takes but a single night! In one night all
these are made, all these lamellas. That is good
work.

A cruel dilemma arises here. Work transforms, and
sometimes destroys, nature. The dilemma is that we
need it undestroyed and untransformed by man if it is
to serve as an ideal, a source of norms, for our work. It
is, perhaps, more difficult now than it was in Keats's

day, or Emerson's or even Rodin's or Juan Ramón's, to find in the book of nature lessons about our work. Somewhere in our subconscious is an idea that nature has become a little too much like us and can no longer be the "something else"—the book written by someone else—that we can learn from. We are too involved in it to draw lessons from it. Juan Ramón, for whom rhythm was one of the deepest secrets of poetry and work, could see, even in the 1940s, that the rhythms of nature were becoming *ours*:

> What do I care about three annual crops of Califor-
> nia apples, which taste like wood, when I have an-
> other Spanish apple, which takes a year to develop
> its juices?

Writers on bioethics remind us, sensibly, that the "us and it" distinction is false: that man, too, is part of nature, part of a "community of living things." But our role has begun to seem too large. We speak fatuously of "managing the environment" (not "nature" but the "environment," the suburbs and surroundings of mankind!). As Bill McKibben taught in *The End of Nature*, the changes we have wrought in the natural world, both deliberately and accidentally, make all of its patterns suspect. A June snowfall or a stunning sunset arouse not a sense of wonder but a sense of doom and guilt. Because man has been monkeying with the climate, every prodigy seems traceable to our intervention: a reflection of our work rather than a norm for it. Nature is less a "given" than it was to Sidney or Bacon, and it is the bioengineer, rather than the poet, who offers to change the "brazen" world into a golden one (page 82).

We can remember, however, that the idea of nature, like religion, has always been a creation of the imagination; that it has sprung from the minds of poets; and that even in Emerson's day, it was an elusive part of reality. Nature is always "elsewhere," he wrote.

> What splendid distance, what recesses of ineffable pomp and loveliness in the sunset! But who can go where they are, or lay his hand or plant his foot thereon? Off they fall from the round world forever and ever.

Nature is *still* elsewhere. We need it for our work, but must work a little harder to evoke it. It is not outside us, but within, this idea of pristine nature—of a process that is not ours but can provide "spiritual norms" for our work. Within us is still an idea of all that is *not* us: the breeze, a bird, the constellations ("golden summits of the darkness"), as in Juan Ramón's proud credo of poetic freedom:

This is my life, the one above,
the pure breeze,
the last bird,
the golden summits of the darkness.

This is my freedom: to smell the rose,
slice the cold water with my crazy hand,
strip the poplar grove,
and steal from the sun its eternal light.

C.M.

Roots and wings. But let the wings take root and the roots take flight.

Observe natural phenomena and you will find in them an inexhaustible source of spiritual norms.

The sea, full of animal, vegetable, and mineral detritus and that of gods, and where we nonetheless bathe in pure water, is an excellent norm for everything else in our lives.

I met someone who had so forgotten clear water that he thought it was a cosmetic.

O critic of my being, is there anything more artificial, more artistic than the work of water and earth, fire and air? Unconscious nature works only with art, the art of work, which she never enunciates but only learns, deafly and dumbly, one century after another, in the dark. And it is we who call ourselves men who can consciously appreciate the depth of that art.

What deceives man, in his appreciation, is that the artificial work of nature is given to him already "done," and he has grown accustomed to this age-old fact, and thus thinks it natural and effortless. Whereas he has to do his own work in a hurry and with critical consciousness . . .

What people call artificial is anything clumsy, false, lightweight; but this is what they ought to call natural. What is really artificial and natural is the slow, the true, the wise; it is *this* that is like nature.

And what chagrin it would cause nature if she could know that she has given birth to the shallow, hurried, critical person rather than to the slow—I mean the artificial—tree.

You hear people say "go to nature" and "leave your books." But one shouldn't go to books only to see nature copied (in some it is a mere pretext) but to see art, which is no less "natural" than nature.

People often praise something for being "imperfect, like nature." But we shouldn't forget that nature is imperfect because unconscious. If it were conscious, it would be perfect.

When we evoke the rose as an example of simplicity, we don't often think of the centuries nature took to create it.

To those who ask why we often make things that are delicate and subtle, etc. — "useless" things — I reply that nature provides an example.

What crystallization, what iridescence, what harmonies are stylized by nature! And within ourselves, the eyes, hands, feet, lips, fingers, the most expressive parts of us, aren't they prodigies of refinement and subtlety?

So why must the rough be more "human" than the refined, as rough people think? And why allege that these exquisite things are artificial? Is a butterfly artificial, a seashell, a tiny wildflower? Are mountains any more natural than these? And if a wildflower is natural, why should it be "delicate" and "unnatural" to copy it?

Doesn't a meteor have the same beauty as a mountain? In the day, I prefer the fugitive, almost invisible meteor; at night, the almost invisible mountain.

Why should it be more beautiful, more meritorious to make the word a cobblestone rather than a flame? Because the flame passes and the stone endures? No. The cobblestone can obstruct, and the flame knows how to hide.

Shadow doesn't leave a spot.

This idea that granite is more consistent and solid than a bee! But beauty isn't measured with the fist. It is measured with the strength of our awareness.

All the world is naked and it creates man naked. Ay! Only man gets dressed, and wants to dress the world!

A feeling for the artificially immense is depriving the world of its feeling for the naturally grand.

Artificial immensity is only the sum of artificial smallness; the naturally grand includes the naturally small, but is not its sum.

An intimate garden, and through the foliage, great horizons, the sea.

Among all trees, the eternal green pine. Among all landscapes, red stone against a blue sky, with white clouds. (And the sea; or better, the feeling that the sea is near.)

"Natural" art. Aesthetic creation shouldn't be forced with any stimulus, either physical or intellectual (coffee, readings, tobacco, wine, trips, the hour); it should be the spontaneous issue of clear, current life.

I imagine my writing as a true sea, because it is made from innumerable waves; as a true sky, because it is made from innumerable stars; as a true desert, because it is made from innumerable grains of sand.

And like the sky, the sea, the desert, it is always in motion and in change.

I think that the most perfect formal and spiritual norm for the artist—light, idea, color, matter, feeling—is the star.

If we look at a star, it seems perfect at each moment: an enchanting, mysterious star. But it is successive, it is always making itself, always traveling toward itself, toward its possibility or its impossibility . . .

To die uncorrupted, like the day and the night.

A diamond with the coolness and freshness of grass.

Violet steel.

If you cannot be gold, be silver. But not silver with gold plate.

I represent our world as an immense, total rose of fire, stone, water, and air, carrying in its bosom forms of surprising, unique, absolute beauty.

The rose, is it geometrical?

How alien to their meaning and to their name: the rose and the nightingale!

Barnyard Fowl

When you learn of someone who speaks ill of the nightingale, go and see. You will surely find a starling or a hen.

She asked me, "Why the rose and not the carnation?"

I answered, "Because the rose is woman, and I, man."

When we used to offer flowers to my mother, she would always answer, "A wild rose, and only one."

I have never forgotten that, nor will I ever. It is my norm.

Two roses are two; four, four; seven, seven. Many, one.

Man should consider himself fortunate to have been a contemporary of the rose.

Time

All that now exists in the world (oceans, fleas, sun, sand, bones, people) has exactly the same age: the age of the world.

White cloud:
broken wing (whose?)
unable to arrive (where?).

Thank you, god. I'm not sure why. But thank you.

No matter how much men discover, they will never make it possible for us to leave this earth of ours. So let us think that here we have everything, that here we will come to an end and be indefinitely reborn; and let us, the living and the dead, feel immense affection for this round, poor world: our father, son, daughter, brother, lover.

Instinct

Sooner or later, any poetics, including a "poetics of work," tries to mediate between two inner forces that govern creation: the rational and the irrational. They are sometimes imagined as working in synchrony, but more often as separate phases in the creative process. A moment of instinctive, passive discovery is followed by one of voluntary reflection. One finds by chance, and then decides what to do with the findings.

"Instinct and intelligence" are the words Juan Ramón uses to describe the relation of spontaneity and reflectiveness. Other poets have spoken of other dichotomies: the conscious and the unconscious, feeling and thinking, inspiration and imagination, the Apollonian and the Dionysian. For Juan Ramón, perfect work comes when these two forces—whatever their names—are in perfect equilibrium. There can be no creative work without instinct, but a wholly instinctive artist would be, for him, a wholly irresponsible one.

Often one of the two is given special privileges. Some poets—Poe explaining how he composed "The Raven," or his disciple Valéry lecturing ironically on the making of his *Cimetière marin*—have chosen to depict their work as a series of deliberate choices, a purely voluntary exercise in which scarcely anything is left to chance. "The talk of inspiration is sheer nonsense," William Morris once wrote. "There is no such thing. It is a mere matter of craftsmanship." What Poe set out to prove in his essay on "The Raven" was that "no one point in its composition is referable either to accident or intuition—that the work proceeded, step by step, to its completion with the precision and rigid consequence of a mathematical problem." A writer weighs the pros and cons of a certain genre, form, or word, and comes to a "rational" solution. Here is Valéry:

> I seek a word (says the poet) a word which is
> feminine,
> has two syllables,
> contains p or f,
> ends in a mute vowel . . .

So much for writing "instinctively"! But perhaps those deliberations came along after the fact. First Chance and then Choice, limping along behind. We are in the late adolescence of Romanticism and rebel against turning work—poetry, copywriting, design—into a series of deliberative acts. Something tells us that art and life are often random; that in art, as in life, we often attribute to deliberation what really arose from circumstance and impulse. And how strong, how resistant to chance, is intelligence, anyway? García Lorca warned, "Intelligence is often the enemy of poetry, because it limits too much, and it elevates the poet to a sharp-edged throne where he forgets that ants could eat him or that a great arsenic lobster could fall on his head."

In Juan Ramón's writing, as in Lorca's (both were Romantics), it is *instinct* that enjoys special privileges. He isn't entirely sure what instinct *is*. And he knows that it is not always the enemy of intelligence: some intelligent people are "instinctively" so. On the whole, however, he wants to make intelligence—that "dirty owl"—more attentive to instinct, more respectful and patient with its finds. He wants to teach intelligence to be a little more humble, both in work and in daily life. For in life, too, we can transform instinct, "through education and culture, into superior insight." As for "blind intelligence," when it is not led by instinct, it does not "serve to guide a man through his world, but can only help him to understand it." Instinct gives us a line of poetry—it gives us anything new at all, a design for a book jacket or a notion about human behavior—"and intelligence must work hard to comprehend it." Work hard not to laugh enviously at it or coax it into looking normal. As always—as happens with remembering and forgetting—achieving "complete" perfection is, to Juan Ramón, a matter of balance. When instinct opens up like a large, strange plant, intelligence knows what to feed it and where to transplant it.

Instinct guides work but is also summoned by work: by concentration, receptivity, and the desire for perfection. Rilke tells that Rodin's concentration was so prodigious

> that he shrugs off the imputation of inspiration, and claims that there is no such thing—no inspiration, but rather only labor—[and] then one suddenly comprehends that to this creator receptivity has become so continuous that he no longer feels its coming, because it is no longer ever absent.

And these stern words from Tchaikovsky: "Inspiration is a guest that does not willingly visit the lazy."

C.M.

. . . Inspiration is like a momentary spark from a more perfect—and, perhaps, more enduring—life. It is like a window of the soul open to a possible existence, an equanimous life which exists in theory, and which we could get to in the depths of our spirit.

I believe in inspiration, but don't trust it very much.

Life gets along well with the unconscious. But as soon as we confront her with our thought, oh how—with how many weapons: noise, cold, pain, heat—she defends herself!

So that my whole self can be content with my work, I need my conscious half to refine, measure, define, and fix what my subconscious has created.

If my work were to make itself, without any effort on my part, I would like it very little; if I were to make it alone, without any will on *its* part, I would like it even less.

There are men whose intelligence can be called instinct, and other, irrational ones whose instinct can be called intelligence (supposing that instinct and intelligence are but degrees of a single power).

Instinct, where is the strength, the wisdom, the magic that can isolate you?

How many shy little things brought to light by intuition have been explained and sanctioned condescendingly by jealous intelligence!

She Gets Even

Intelligence usually dominates instinct. But instinct, which is older than intelligence and also younger — for it is permanent — knows how to get even. How few times the dirty owl of intelligence escapes from instinct's terrible, clean beak! And yet, how few times Venus comes completely out of the sea, virgin and pure, in her own special manner.

Intelligence usually tramples on the flowers of instinct, but ah, when it cannot!

There is a place within us that can be reached by intelligence. But there is a deeper one that only the spirit can get to. And that is why those who are "merely completely intelligent" — in science or art, verse or prose — always seem like spies.

Let our intelligence keep a watch on our instinct. But let us give it enough freedom so that the child can do a little — more than a little — of what it wants.

Intelligence isn't there to guide instinct but to comprehend it.

Our instinct is constantly correcting us. And if we follow its correction, after having thought about it, we will lose nothing and gain much.

More than conscious creation, deft criticism of the spontaneous.

People think that reflection destroys the work that is felt. No, no: feeling knows how to defend herself from thought, like a woman from a man, keeping him where he belongs.

Feel ideas acutely, and meditate slowly upon sentiment.

Don't feel ashamed of your basest instinct . . . lead it like a blind man, tame it like a beast, love it as you would an inferior self.

Norms, disciplines? Whims, tastes.

If they give you lined paper, write the other way . . .

Caprice and crucible.

Dream

Dreams tempt us with their wealth. They are our imaginative endowment, the mind's unspent capital. Most of us are content to live on the interest. But many books that promise to awaken our "creativity" argue for the usefulness of dreaming. In a few easy steps, they say, we can "incubate" our dreams and learn to decipher, remember, and apply them better. We can select a problem and pose it to our dreams as a question: "How can I become more confident?"

Juan Ramón encourages us to do the opposite: rejoice that dreaming cannot be turned into a "productive" form of labor, of problem solving. In dreams and in reverie, work lies fallow. Our will—to finish, to solve the problem—is suspended. Something that is not the will takes over and alters the unconscious, juxtaposing images that we could not have brought together during our waking hours. And often, in blissful passivity or terrifying helplessness, something emerges into the conscious mind—not exactly the solution to a problem, or even an idea, but something more vague. In his dreams Juan Ramón was aware only of "colors, planes, lights, positions in time and space," or the vague feeling of something having happened:

I have a feeling that my boat
has struck, down there in the depths,
against a great thing. And nothing
happens! Nothing . . . Silence . . . Waves . . .

Nothing happens! Or has everything happened,
and we are standing now, quietly, in the new life?

(Translation by Robert Bly)

Poems and aphorisms about dreams and reverie are everywhere in his work. Juan Ramón regards dreams not as a curiosity but with deep reverence, and always from a certain distance. For him, dreams are *not* a way of discovering information about his work or about himself. As he bends over the water, he sees beyond his own distorted reflection into depths that have, apparently, nothing to do with him at all. Dreams attract him, like nature, precisely because they are *not* him, because they allow him a glimpse of another order of things. He would agree with the French philosopher Gaston

Bachelard that in dreams we are removed from ourselves:

> The night dream does not belong to us. It is not our possession. With regard to us, it is an abductor, the most disconcerting of abductors: it abducts our being from us. [In the deepest dreams] we are returned to an ante-subjective state. We become elusive to ourselves . . .

Nor does Juan Ramón wish to "apply" his dreams to his work. He is doubtful he can capture the language of dreams in his writing, and although he speaks often of the pleasures of dreaming, few of his poems are the narration of actual dreams. He does not believe, as some psychologists do, in translating the language of dreams into that of reality, and he knows that there are dream strata "below our lives and above our deaths" that neither the psychologist nor the poet will ever get at. Following a long tradition of Spanish poets—the best known is Calderón de la Barca—he affirms that, when the play of life is over, what is "lived" is indistinguishable from what is "dreamt." Idealists like Juan Ramón can never easily decide which of these two halves of our lives is the "real" one. Some of his poems make us feel that we are flying at night, upside down, unable to know whether those lights are coming from the stars or from an earthly city. He believes fervently in the restorative, healing power of dreams: they are the "madness" that keeps us sane; the poetry that chastens our reality; something unbalanced that gives equilibrium to the working day. They purify what happened the day before.

Thought that can't climb over the fence at night . . . leave it in the henhouse of evening.

For him, there is always a jolting moment of disillusionment when he returns to the "false gold" of day. From the verge of his dream, he can hear his work beckoning (his syntax here still wobbles in its sleep):

The poem calls to me, like love, from its place. I go to it in the order of new today, different continuation of new yesterday; go to the written page, which catches the reflection—hard atmosphere over a white river, through the rigid glass of the window— the gray already blue of the sky and the already green of the tree.

In the "false gold" of morning, he walks along an imaginary beach, looking for what has been left there by the tides of dream. He picks up "only what glows in the dawn." He does not stop for the driftwood collected by surrealists. The notion of "automatic writing"—the dictation taken down from dream—runs counter to his notion of the poet as "above all, responsible." If there is a lesson for work to be drawn from his thoughts on dreaming, it is this: dream toward the spirit and not toward reality, and let your dreams alone. They are the part of you that, happily, you cannot control. They are all that is not your work. By themselves, without training or coercion, they will remind you of your limits, carry you outside them, and refresh you in your daily labor.

C.M.

I want to look at things, but only see through them.

Sometimes my daydreams follow one another so quickly and abundantly that I think I am bleeding to death.

> There is a me who is sleeping
> —buzzing fly of an idea!—
> and there is a me who is staying awake
> so I won't go to sleep.

Prolong your reverie past sunset into the night.

Riches of night, how many secrets taken from you, how many yet to take, though none of them is your secret or mine, night!

What unspeakable pleasure, to plunge my hand deep into you, stirring your stars!

Luminous touch of other hands searching for your treasures!

I can pluck more from dream than from life, for dream is like a better life, whose roses I would like to plant in my reality.

. . . In our dreams, memory makes us "sane with blackness," and this seems a natural state for us; more natural, at least, than to be "crazy with light."

Let us dream whatever we want, for when life and dream are gone, a thing lived is no different from a thing dreamt.

Dreams trap me like cobwebs in bloom. I must break free of them, because if I didn't, the nuances of things would drive me crazy.

I sing my dreams to sleep like a mother singing to her crying children.

Not to dream? But dream is the prelude, the main-spring of action; and the best, most beautiful action is the one dreamt of!

Yes, let us learn from our sleep and our dreams to look at life. That is enough.

Thought that can't climb over the fence of night . . . leave it in the henhouse of evening.

Dream toward the spirit, never toward reality, for reality will spring from your heart.

I dreamt I was dead and that, dead, I was dreaming that I was coming back to life and could not. And I dreamt that that dream would be eternal.

What a shame to awaken now, just as I was finding in the life of dream what I had lost in the dream of life.

Dream, My Treasure

Every morning I wake up bankrupt.

How very sad! Last night I learned the origin of things and was at the center of the secret of the universe. I was the possessor of all the highest reasons for our existence, and *now, what*? The fiery nightmare of "life," the tragic, ugly sun of people hawking their wares in nasal voices, and of carpets being beaten.

How tired my whole body feels, abandoned by its royal guest. And how long it takes, poor thing, to resign itself to the "natural" blood pressure that propels it once again toward false things—the pressure that wide-awake doctors call "normal," and that is felt in one's pulse and reflexes: signs that vile man has been thrown out of timeless dream into the teeming waiting room of three o'clock . . . !

In the morning I sweep up the fallen leaves of my dreams as the gardener sweeps away the dry leaves.

Awakening

For you, life,
I want, always, to be the flower
that closes its petals

and gathers the treasure of night,
opening them to the day,
to give the entire essence
of its dream.

Every morning when I go to the beach of yesterday, I pick up only what has been purified at night by the sea, only what glows in the dawn.

Awakenings are usually sad, for life catches us without warning, after the treasures of dream . . . And thus the morning is something like a ruin. And then thought and light begin adapting to one another, and we get that miserable fictitious structure called "day," false gold. Simulacrum of a great, beautiful life that must exist someplace else . . .

Dream is the atmosphere of superior reality from which we emerge molded and modeled every morning for a new physical and moral impulse: the true lodging along our magical road, a stopping place foreseen, day after day, on the way to our final destination.

If we could learn to catch it by surprise, the word from our dreams could be our best and truest.

Nocturnal Language

The word of dream, nocturnal language, is other than itself.

To put it differently: when we awake, what we usually believe we were saying in our dreams isn't usually what we were saying, even if, out of haste, indifference, boredom, or forgetfulness, it *seems* to be the same and satisfies us.

In the state between sleep and wake, just before we awaken, on the very border of ourselves, standing on the bank, as though changing languages at the frontier, we do a subconscious or unconscious translation of the word of dream: a strange, subtle exchange which differs from itself as greatly as a nude which we dream of differs in color, touch, charm, and mystery differs from the nude of reality.

They are two and they are one. Two in one, as we ourselves are.

It is good to balance the sadness of losing a dream or an idea with the joy of some work that has been realized.

Sleepless

Night goes away, black bull (dense flesh of mourning, fright, and mystery) that has bellowed terrible and immense, making all the fallen sweat with fear, and day comes, fresh child asking trust, love, and laughter (child who, far away, in the hidden places where beginnings meet endings, has played for a moment on I know not what prairie of light and shadow with the bull that was fleeing).

Above and Below Our Death

The dreams we dream are deposited in the depths of our being, as in the successive depths of a mine. The first level can be found easily when we awaken: light dreams, a blanket of foam, fleeting sadness or happiness. It takes more effort to find the second one, under its thick fur. Perhaps sometime we will find the third one, coming upon it by surprise. The fourth . . . has a double or quadruple layer . . . And suddenly there is another level that we can't even glimpse, deep down in its lair, without any relation to us at all.

We live and die at one, two, three meters below "our earth." In "our earth" everything that is "ours" happens to us, even "our" dreams. Somebody or something has placed that final level at his or its own level, that stratum which we will never be able to excavate and which remains, always, beneath our life and forever above our death . . .

I have dreamt my life and lived my dream.

[Prayer]

O dream, you who are the truth, or a simulacrum of the truth; who give us strength to return to the falsehood of the world and who hold the key to each day of the future; who have no balance, but balance the senses and the will; who are the madness that keeps us sane and the poetry that makes our reality: brush me with your large sweet wings; open my eyes inward into myself; still the murmuring in my ears; and make me see the light I cannot see and the melody I cannot hear.

Death

Why *death* in a book about work? Who but a poet would want death reading over his shoulder?

Even the thought of death can bring work to a standstill. Juan Ramón's fellow poet Unamuno liked to quote the anonymous Spanish song:

> When I remember I must die,
> I lay my cape upon the floor
> and get my fill of sleep.

And yet, because death is the end of our worklife, the thought of death can also be a stimulus. The approach of evening and night alters the tempo and rhythm of our work, and changes what we give our attention to. The struggle to produce enduring work is a consolation for, and a distraction from, and a vivid protest against, our mortality. Through our work, if it is important enough to us, we leave something truly *ours* for those who will follow:

Work

> Yes, for how little time.
> And yet, because each moment
> can be my eternity,
> what a unique little time.

Good work perpetuates us, consoles us for the fleetingness of life. Unamuno insists, "Work is the only *practical* consolation we have for having been born."

Juan Ramón was always worrying—always consulting his doctors—about whether he would have enough time to revise, "definitively" arrange, and publish the best that he had written. Each day, he conjured up his death, reminding himself, his wife, and his friends that he had been born with a weak heart and cursing its arrhythmia for interrupting the rhythm of his daily labor. The thought of death gains special meaning to those like him who conceive of their work not as a series of tasks—for these can be left to others—but as a whole. In the evening he would often measure the time he thought he had left against the work that was left to do.

> My entire work is well organized now. Not in vain have I worked my whole life, without stopping for a

single day, and if I could have just another ten years to live, and could just leave my work finished, I wouldn't mind having it placed beside that of anyone else, from any period, from any country. But one of these days an artery pops, and it is all over. I would, at least, like to work until I'm sixty: I think one can still work fully at sixty; more than that, I don't know . . . And so my norm these days is to bring things to completion.

It was April of 1934. He lived another twenty-four years, and died at age seventy-seven. Among the hundred thousand manuscript pages in the archives are the outlines of many unpublished books—memos to posterity—from which the late Antonio Sánchez Romeralo and other scholars have tried to piece together his glorious unfinished quilt: his *Obra.*

For him, to remember death was also to remember the "eternity" he wanted for his work: "I think so much about death because I know that when I am dead, I am going to live more than I did when alive." Death, he thought, would complete him, closing the circle—the orbit or zero—of his life (page 139).

Light and Shadow

I will not be me, death, until you come together with my life and bring me to completion; not until my half of light is closed with my half of shadow and

I can be eternal balance in the mind of the world:
sometimes, the half-self that is radiant; and sometimes, the other that is oblivion . . .

Death was his constant companion and source of inspiration; it was, together with his beloved wife and his
"expression," one of his three muses. Death as muse!
His disciple García Lorca took that thought deeply to
heart and said that without a constant, intense awareness of death, no real inspiration is possible. For Lorca,
"every step that a man climbs in the tower of his own,
personal perfection" is taken by struggling with a
deathly force, the earth spirit he personified as the
duende. One's life and work can have style, grace,
beauty, a certain captivating *je ne sais quoi*, and yet,
without the *duende*—the playful, ineffable, and somewhat diabolical goblin that feeds on our awareness of
death—there can be no deep inspiration, no work that
can truly move others, baptizing them, time after time,
"in dark water." The *duende*, Lorca tells us, struggles
with the creator "on the very rim of the well," on the
lips of a wound that never heals. He does not come at
all unless he knows that death is somewhere close by.
The creator must acknowledge that he is mortal, and
"the *duende* must know beforehand that he can serenade
death's house and rock those branches we all wear,
branches that do not have, will never have, any consolation." Those "branches," obviously, are our mortality.

One of Juan Ramón's favorite ideas—so that the thought of death would neither stop him in his tracks nor make his work unbearable—was that death is already a familiar presence in our lives and therefore not to be feared. That perception was an old one in Spanish poetry. Centuries earlier, Francisco de Quevedo—a prodigious worker prodigiously afraid of death—calmed himself with the thought that death is already "inside" us, already part of us even before we leave the womb:

> Before it learns to walk the foot is spurring
> down the road toward death.

Life, in Quevedo's nihilistic equation, is "living death." If it "is" at all, it is a "nothing that, being, is little, and will be nothing." Death isn't something that comes to us from afar, from someplace outside ourselves, out of the future or the past. It is already here. Quevedo came to imagine himself as a "present succession of the dead." Entombed within him were the child, the youth, the man he had once been: an image to which Juan Ramón returns in one of his aphorisms. He is "a sepulchre full of all my dead." But Juan Ramón treats death more tenderly and intimately than either Lorca or Quevedo. What was there to fear from such a quiet, familiar presence?

What happens to music
when it ceases to be sound, and what
to a breeze that ceases
to flutter, and what
to a light that ceases to burn?

Death, tell me, what are you but silence,
calm, shadow?

C.M.

All my life, in every place, every day, in every light and color; asleep and awake, happy and sad, poor and rich, I have felt death by my side. I'm beginning to think that she likes having me as a living friend.

What an obsession with death! The earth seems to be waiting for me, sadly, as for a prodigal son.

Why are the dead so heavy? Is it because when we are alive the spirit feels the pull of the luminous heavens? Is it because flesh without soul is only collapse and ruin? Ah, the heaviness of the dead!

The yawn: anticipation of the tomb! Taste of the earth of the dead, entering the gut!

What does death matter if, in life and in work, we have conquered it day after day; if we have gone beyond it in our thoughts and our hearts?

Why this fear of death if, from the infinite origin of the world until our birth, we were in death so pleasantly, and have such lovely memories of what went before our accidental, momentary existence between two eternities?

Perhaps this momentary life of ours is only the light that divides our infinite origin from our infinite end?

To die, what we call dying, is not to die but only to die another time.

Every morning we emerge from the grave.

> Ah, sleep,
> how we learn in you to die!

> With what magisterial beauty
> you lead us, through gardens
> that seem more and more ours,
> to the great knowledge of the dark!

I am nothing more than a sepulchre full of all my dead; and my tomb will simply be another me.

To live is nothing more than to come here to die, to be what we were before being born, but with apprenticeship, experience, knowledge of cause, and perhaps with will.

The worst thing about death must be the first night.

Dear wife, to return to nothing will be like going back to our little house after a short or a long trip through this foreign life.

As with life, one is dead for a certain period only. We might say that death lasts no longer than life. After seventy or eighty years of earth, we are no longer dead, just as we are no longer alive after seventy or eighty years of life.

Death is no longer than life. Ten years of life, ten of death; thirty, thirty; eighty, eighty.

First nonbeing; then birth; then life; then death; then nonbeing.

"To be" dead is "to be." Being. Life.

Death isn't eternal either. (Nonbeing kills it.)

Life kills nonbeing; death kills life; nonbeing kills death. To be born, live, die. Three airy episodes in nonbeing.

Epitaph
I have only the life you give me. Remember me!

I think so much about death because I know that when I am dead, I am going to live more than I did when alive.

Orbits, Zeros, Graves
Our orbit is a zero; a line and a void. And all we do is draw that zero each minute, hour, day, week, month, year. If we stumble, the zero is a grave.

If today I am seventy years old, how many zeros have I drawn around the zero of the sun? Into how many graves have I tumbled?

All of space is full of orbits, zeros, and infinite mystery. Immense orbit, immense zero.

All of creation: immense zero to be stumbled into, immense grave!

Add it up.

Writing

Writing

Writing is work and the record of work and a way to make ourselves fully conscious of our work. The effort to write and work perfectly is a way of pursuing form and eluding death, the end of form.

Juan Ramón reminds us that in order to create that form—to create our own form in writing—we must slow down and bring it lovingly into existence:

First, the word itself: an island. Next, the blissful joining, as in love, of two words. Later, finally, the whole period, like a world both closed and open . . .

He suggests that only what is made slowly and lovingly can last. And what if, despite our loving effort, the writing does *not* last? Juan Ramón marveled over the frailness of his medium: "Beauty on a sheet of paper! To live even a little, you must elude fire, support the air, escape from water, and cheat the earth!" Even if his manuscripts endured, surviving mold and fire, the chaos of war and of life in exile, who would need and remember his writing? Who would take pleasure in it? That thought helped him to dwell in the present, to forget posterity ("Such haste to be eternal!"), and to rejoice in writing for its own sake. When we try to write perfectly, we write not to please the future but to *please ourselves*:

> This or that person says to me, "Why this eagerness, this insistence, this ecstasy over your work?"
>
> I answer with this delicious poem of Abū Saʿīd, the Persian:
>
> I asked my beloved, "Why do you make yourself beautiful?"
>
> "To please myself," she answered. "Because there are moments when I am, at the same time, the mirror and the woman looked at, and beauty itself; moments when I feel that I am, at the same time, love, and the lover, and the beloved."

In his advice about writing, Juan Ramón tells us that perfection lies in equilibrium. He wants to balance brevity and fullness; spontaneity and exactness; the rare word and the common one; the wish to control his own meaning, and the ability to let go and trust that the reader will find others.

His ideal is simplicity and freshness. He wants his writing to be succulent as a fruit, tight as a seed. "Not a walnut, not an odorless dahlia." He recoils from archaism, rhetoric, padding: all these belong to "literature," and for him, "literature" and "poetry" are at opposite poles of writing. Literature is voluntary and complicated, while poetry is instinctive and simple:

> Literature is decorative, ingenious, external, because it is created by comparing, commenting, and copying. Literature is translation; poetry, original. If poetry is for deep feelings, literature is for superficial ones. Poetry is instinctive—terse and easy like a fruit or a flower. It comes in one piece. But literature, in its struggle to "incorporate" the external, is "worked over," juxtaposed, Baroque.

These words, from a lecture, allude to, and exemplify, an inner struggle. Juan Ramón struggled, in his own words, with a "Baroque architect with a full stomach" who wanted to take over his writing. Among his papers, saved by chance from the "kaleidoscope" of his wastebasket, we find symmetrical "Baroque" fragments like this one:

> Give the women in your life all that you want to, know how to, and can. Accept from them all that they can, know how to, and want to give you. And

don't be occupied or preoccupied with what they want, know how to, or can give to others . . .

Perfect writing is otherwise. It is "naked." Poetry can wear sandals, but never shoes. In all perfect writing, the form is there, but it is invisible "like the current of a river," and the form and "accent" are one's own.

Unamuno once said that perfect work—be it the work of a shoemaker or a civil servant—seems irreplaceable because it is unique. He spoke of work so good that through it the worker makes his own death seem an inconsolable insult, an outrage. The same applies to writing. That aura of uniqueness is known as style. For Juan Ramón, style is not a matter of linguistic idiosyncrasy. "Style is not the pen, and not the language." It isn't the "juggling act" of that hateful Baroque architect. To find one's style is to find "the exact, the only expressive path for our being . . . the unbreakable thread in our living labyrinth. Our inexhaustible and pleasurable current." And this is true of all good work. When we find the right work, we find the "path for our being." It gives our lives a "current." In the thought of Juan Ramón, writing is an image of work, and work is an image of writing: they are the fleeting form we try to leave upon the earth.

C.M.

First, the word itself: an island. Next, the blissful joining, as in love, of two words. Later, finally, the whole period, like a world both closed and open, containing (within itself, within itself alone) the infinite.

What matters in writing, I think, is that the ordinary word seems to be used for the first time, and the rare one seems ordinary, so that one doesn't stumble over it, and no word feels strange or wrong, wherever it is placed.

Defending an "approximate" poetic writer, another half-writer said, "It's just that we don't want to find the exact word but the approximate one."

"Yes to both of you," I said, "but the word which *isn't* quite right, that one too must be found, and found exactly."

In poetry, the word should be so exact that the reader forgets it and only the idea remains: a little like a river that makes us forget the water and remember only the current.

Useless to be prodigal with words. They only acquire their true meaning when they are well applied. To call someone mediocre "illustrious" is like calling a thistle "soft" or a star "black." The ideas don't cohere, the concepts don't come together.

May my word be the thing itself, newly created by my soul. And may all who do not know them go through me to things; and all who forget them go through me to things; and all who love them go through me to things. Intelligence, give me the exact name—your name, and theirs, and my own name—of things!

One must speak in such a way that although someone else, or many others, or an infinite number of people, have said it before, it seems as though you said it first.

You can repeat a word in writing or speech as often as necessary. Repeating the exact word is no defect, no poverty. The synonyms are there for all to see in the dictionary.

The value of repetition depends on who does the repeating.

Never copy yourself.

Say it differently, but let it seem natural.

There are those who repeat unconsciously what another says (extreme imperfection). And those who repeat it consciously. Those who consciously do not repeat it. And those who unconsciously do not repeat it (extreme perfection).

Rhetoric produces in me the loathing for anything that is hatefully useless, like sleeplessness late at night, like a medicine taken when we are healthy, like a lamp burning in the daytime, like a bed still made in the morning.

The annihilation of form through the perfection of form.

Formal perfection (simplicity, spontaneity) is neither rambling carelessness nor the juggling act of some Baroque architect with a stuffed belly. In both cases, one gets tangled up in form, and at every moment it demands our attention and makes us stumble. It is, rather, the absolute exactitude that makes form disappear, leaving only the content. So that the form *is* the content . . .

The perfection of artistic form lies not in its celebration but in its disappearance . . .

A horror of archaism. Pure present, fresh and agreeable.

I cannot conceive of a god who is an orator.

No deep truth has ever been shouted.

How frightful, the house, the soul when empty—or full—of words.

A good, true, beautiful word soothes more than any sedative.

Poetry is the almost said, literature the said, rhetoric the re-said. The almost said is the highest category of beauty.

When he speaks very badly or too well, man seems irrational, a pig or a canary. He only seems a man when he expresses himself in his sufficient, daily language.

But "daily" here means so much! I think that if God were to speak, he would speak in ordinary language, making mistakes at times.

Padding

In rhymed verse, it is what you would not say in free verse; in free verse, what you would not say in ordinary prose; in ordinary prose, what you would not say were you speaking exactly.

Much, yes, as long as it is as good as little.

The greatest of everything and of nothing has needed names no longer than: be, sun, faith, no, sea, light, yes, today, God, peace, voice, thirst, more, war.

To get it right, go back to the words of your mother.

Write the way you speak and you will go further and be more spoken of than by writing the way you write.

Rare intuition and the common word: the greatest possible beauty.

Words, like waves and wings, are always virgin.

It matters nothing that the ideas we enunciate seem wrong for the time and place. No matter how isolated and abstract they seem to us, they will come into their meaning, with a huge variety of unsuspected nuances, when the reader finds himself in a moral situation analogous to the one in which they were written.

When you express yourself, try it at different times of the day, in different lights, and, if possible, in different places. Even, if possible, among different people.

Forget the high, fixed northern light that so many painters longed for.

I believe that when people speak of style, they generally confuse substance with what is secondary. When they speak of style, they speak of the word, and I believe that style is something which comes from the bottom of the soul. That is the drift of my aphorisms.

Style: the exact, the only expressive path for our being, the definitive discovery of the unbreakable thread in our living labyrinth. Our inexhaustible and pleasurable current.

Style: the path of someone with land, the current of someone with sea or river, the thread of someone with labyrinth.

Let us not doodle uselessly in the margins of reality.

The word is made, was made, for the ear, not the eye. And poetry comes in more at the ear than at the eye.

When we feel the impulse to write, let us not reason whether or not we ought to write this or that, but simply write it, for to write is to create. And later we can reason whether or not to "save" it.

Friend, do not think about what has been lost of what you have written, but about what you have not written, which is much more lost for you.

Revision

Revision

Not everyone pursues perfection in writing, but work of all kinds involves a slow, final disposition of details—refining, purifying, polishing—and a moment of thought for how the work will be received.

To revise what we have done or made—to look at it again, slowly and lovingly—is, for some, the most pleasurable phase of work, and one of the deepest pleasures in life. But revision is not merely a matter of looking. The work of "retouching" or "polishing" seems to arise, as Gaston Bachelard once noticed, from a certain primitive libidinal urge. He tells us of the continued "caress" of polishing: its "gentle, rhythmic, seductive movement." Juan Ramón, too, speaks of "caressing" his work and of bestowing perfection on it "like a big round hug." Others have compared revision to maternal love. It was said of Virgil that he gave birth to his poems and then, like a bear, licked them slowly into shape.

Few people fully enjoy that pleasure, and some do it with a machine. In the case of written texts, revision is often left to the spell-checker. A tired student hands me his composition with the comment "I just printed it out . . . I didn't have time to go back over it." The expectation is that *I* will, tidying up after him. His lost pleasure turns into my tedium. I remember Juan Ramón: "How can we expect others to love our work if we do not feel immense love for it ourselves?"

No modern poet can have devoted more thought to revision than he did. For him, creation and correction were the counterpoint of poetry, parts of one same, unending process. His work was always in progress. He came to think that his very earliest books, as books, were beyond salvation, and begged his friends and admirers to bring him copies, purchased at secondhand bookstalls or purloined from the National Library, which he destroyed or pulled apart, saving only the individual pages that might be rewritten and rearranged. Those pages, and other first, or second, or third drafts of poems, sometimes went into boxes in the basement of his Madrid apartment building. They were the subsoil of his daily labor. When space became available, the boxes were carried up to his workroom, where dozens of different books in progress were spread out carefully on the floor and the furniture. He dreamed of a "simple, long, narrow pine table" where he could see before him seventy or eighty books he had already written and could fall, "by surprise," on this or that poem, revise it, and dictate a new version to Zenobia. To publish a poem was sometimes only a way of distancing himself from it: on the printed page, its defects stood out more sharply. Poems that had already appeared in books, poetry magazines, and newspapers were "published drafts"—excellent grist for the mill.

He revised, at first, in his head. But over the years his manner of revision changed. In 1931, for example, his friend Juan Guerrero Ruiz heard him explain

> that he has decided not to do the final revision he used to do while lying on the sofa and working from memory, analyzing each text, one word after another, until leaving it completely finished. This used to involve a huge amount of mental work, and [he thinks that] perhaps it left the poems too pure, and now he has had a change of thought and understands that it is better to leave things a little unfinished, without that final phase of revision. "Better to leave the work a little fresher, though it be less perfect."

Juan Ramón's best-known poem—

Touch it no more.
The rose is like that.

—suggests that although there is no end to revision, there is a point when revision becomes "sufficient." "Perfect and imperfect, like the rose," he said in an aphorism. In another one, addressed angrily to a critic, he added, "When I say 'touch it no more,' I mean that I have already touched everything, even the rose!" And he was probably right. That little poem may have begun as part of a longer one, and ignoring his own advice, Juan Ramón was to change it again before he died, turning the two lines into one.

What other insights did he acquire, over decades of reflection, about correction and revision? From his aphorisms, we can deduce the following advice:

• *Surprise your work.* Sneak up on it and revise it "by surprise," as though it were the work of someone else. Correct it as though you were a "surprised, intelligent reader" of yourself. Only from a psychological distance will you see your work clearly and take any pleasure in it.

• *Revise part of your work, but remember the whole.* When you correct a single work, you are revising something larger: all the work you have ever done and will ever do. "I revise neither page nor book, but Work." Juan Ramón teaches us that, in revising even a paragraph, we are preparing another "draft" of the work of our entire lives. This kept him from fretting endlessly over nuances.

• *Correction is sometimes only confirmation.* You needn't always change the work, only "relive" it imaginatively, "confirm" it, "hear its confession," and send it on its way.

• *Respect the person you were.* To revise intelligently, you must pardon your former self—whoever it was who wrote *that*!—and try to balance "instinct" and critical intelligence. "Don't strike from your work the word you no longer understand. There was a reason you put it there."

• *Respect the defect that cannot be conquered.* It is an irreducible element of your style, your "character" (see the next chapter).

• *Take down the scaffolding.* Even after intensive revision, finished work should seem fresh and spontaneous, without a trace of the labor that went into it. The Spaniard Lope de Vega, who wrote over a thousand plays, once said he wanted "the rough draft very dark and the ideas very clear." After revising a poem, Juan Ramón liked to destroy the rough draft, "making fun of the future philologist."

Robert Frost, the "sweet gray swan of New England," to whom Juan Ramón refers in some of his essays and aphorisms, once remarked that poems are never finished, only abandoned. The quality of revision depends on the instinct and the intelligence that go into that abandonment, and the thought taken for the people who will *find* the abandoned work: how they will use it, what will become of it. Some poems are abandoned with remorse; others, with boredom or desperation. Juan Ramón wanted to abandon each of his poems with all the intelligence and love that went into their creation.

C.M.

Impossible last week of each work!

This constant struggle between wanting to be finished and wanting to finish well!

Nothing more vain and absurd than to correct with "a will to finish."

To go back over one's work — or not to — is only a problem of love.

How can we expect others to love our work if we do not feel immense love for it ourselves?

No delight you lavish on your work will be wasted on it.

Whoever doesn't relive his work day after day risks having others see in it beauties and secrets that he himself ignores. As though someone else were able to see in our mothers, wives, or daughters what we ourselves were unable to see.

In our work, there can be something we haven't seen, but nothing we haven't looked at.

To create with all the senses of the soul and the body. And to correct with one sense only, that of sight, the eye.

Because what is given to us, intimately, by the god of the moment cannot be corrected. And what remains, when that god has vanished, is only "inspection."

To correct something, return to it suddenly. Catch it stark naked and alone.

When we correct, it should be as if we were intelligent, surprised readers of ourselves.

To correct: find order in surprise.

Surprise

For me, the supreme virtue of life, in the realm both of the useful and of the beautiful, is surprise. To surprise I entrust my destiny, and my destiny expects everything from her and in her.

When revising my poetry, which I am continually stroking and caressing, I've always corrected by means of surprise. Somewhere in my workplace (table, chair, floor) I leave the poem or note I have begun. I look lovingly at it for a moment, without being too hard on it or on myself. And then I go away, taking it away to a spot in true memory . . . For possible expression is everywhere: on the page, in the atmosphere, anyplace in the house. And when I go back to that expression, which is expecting me and which, without a doubt, knows what I am bringing to it, the expression rises up to me and yields up its secret, its life. And thus what I give to the text—or better, what the text gives to me— what we give to each other—is surprise.

One must catch life and death by surprise. Everything beautiful in life and death is best seen that way. Maybe death and life need a method, but the method must be surprising, must be in love with surprise. Technique must be warm, jumpy, vital. Nothing uglier than the unknown but expected face; nothing lovelier than the familiar or strange face caught by surprise.

Surprise leaps over everything and over us with the naked emotion of erect feeling, of spirit.

If one reads (corrects) very slowly, the language comes off its hinges and ends up saying nothing.

Correction can only be rapid and successive. Anything else would paralyze writing.

When one tries too hard with a poem (a painting, a piece of music), it vanishes. Because final, true, invariable, incorrigible perfection is nothingness, is *naða*.

Don't strike from your work the word you no longer understand. There was a reason you put it there.

Any Meaning at All
When we correct our writing, it is enough to find there a meaning: any of the innumerable meanings it can have, although the meaning be different, or have a different nuance, from the one we thought it had when it was created.

Take it from me: there is no greater madness than that of the madman of "nuances."

Successive Axiom

No day . . . without erasing a line and tearing up some paper or other.

No page is too insignificant not to be torn up.

In the papers in my wastebasket, what beauties of rhythm and color! What a restless, dull kaleidoscope!

When you wonder which version is better, don't lose time arguing with yourself. Leave them both.

Savior

We live from, and with, what we save.

He told me, "I write five hundred pages and leave a hundred."

"Not me," I answered. "I write fifty and leave fifty-one and a half."

For me, the world has two parts: one where there might be papers of mine, and one where there are none. How restful, the second!

I would like to live for another year after my death, without the power to create anything new, simply to revise the work I have already completed.

Go back to improve, not to doubt.

A work is fully corrected and purified when we have reread it and relived it, and it gives the full, exact impression of its life at the instant it was created.

To correct is not to exhaust or kill; it is to make complete, to leave the work alive forever.

When correcting myself, I have tried to respect the accent.

Refining a work need not necessarily mean modifying (transforming). A poem can be perfectly refined—and this is frequent in mine—without having undergone the least change. To refine it was only to hear its confession and have the pleasure of finding it (without defects) perfect.

In most cases, my corrections are like a successful second fitting.

Since there is no end to correction, let it simply be sufficient.

Let us not forget that some defects are invincible. It is these that give the defect its perpetuity and prestige. Exactness lies in conquering the six conquerable defects and respecting the seventh, the only invincible one.

What delight: sure of ourselves at last, to relive the work of something beautiful that we have made!

How wonderful it feels, after so much effort, to leave things just the way they were!

Perfection must be given to the work like a big round hug.

What has been well revised in the morning . . . how beautifully "classical" (eternal) it seems in the evening!

Let our work be free of us: the scaffolding taken down, the future philologist made fun of: naked, smooth, and round, like the egg of some bird, like the seed of some plant, like Venus on her shell.

Let the finished book go on quivering with emotion and intelligence, a clean arrow newly and forever fixed into the double tree of life and of art.

Complete: perfect and imperfect in equilibrium.

Perfection

Reflection

J uan Ramón's idea of perfection departs from the common meaning of the word and places more emphasis on process than on product. For him, something perfect is something that is becoming complete and that is nothing but *becoming*: a thing moving slowly and successively into its own, helped along, in the case of art, by instinct and intelligent reflection. Perfection means gradual movement toward an ideal intuited in creative reverie or, as Juan Ramón puts it, in "the well-nourished subconscious." We have spoken of his paradigms of perfection in nature: the star, because, as it burns, it seems to be "always making itself"; and the rose, because it is both perfect and imperfect. The latter two qualities, when in equilibrium, give us the highest norm to which art and work can aspire: plenitude and sensual fullness. Juan Ramón speaks of the "sufficient infinite" of the rose. *Just enough* infinity, just the right dose of "eternity"!

How unbearable eternity would be if it lasted more than one or two or three minutes. As unbearable as a long poem, a mass, a whole night of love, a rosary. Prayer, love, poetry, all of the highest moments in life, are eternal if they are beautiful and fleeting. Eternity is a conception of the wistful, bored person.

Perfection is neither being "completely finished" nor being "totally free of defects." That sort of perfection — what we call "quality" — is, for him, "poison." The defect — when it is a beautiful, fatal gift of inspiration — is what gives an object its own memorable character, rescuing it from sameness. Inconsistency is the enemy of quality, but not of perfection as Juan Ramón conceives of it:

Yes, inconsistent. Like all natural and supernatural forces: water, air, fire, earth, the flesh, light, love, the rose, grace, joy, pain.

In short, perfection is dynamic and successive: a poem or thing in movement toward its plenitude. No wonder that Juan Ramón seized delightedly on an expression he had seen in American and English poets: "work in progress." To him, what is no longer "in progress" can move no one, not even its creator. Something truly perfect gives us the feeling of imminence, of being *about to happen*. Perfection is always being realized, and even when it is abandoned, the perfect poem will continue, always, to "quiver with emotion and intelligence" (see "Revision"). Perfection is approximation. It is "penultimate imperfection," the "always of never." In poetry and in any creative work, there is always another step, leading to boredom and sterility, and it is better not to take it.

C.M.

Simplicity, freshness, purity, sharpness, synthesis . . . perfection.

Perfect, but natural.

The infinitely small, when it reaches a certain point of perfection, is as great as the infinitely large.

Much and perfect. In the *and* lies the secret, the little problem.

"The best is no enemy of the good," says the Spanish proverb. But it is.

Bad is closer to good than is mediocre.

Careful, friends! Every day we confuse rhetoric with perfection.

Perfection: in art, perfection is the fruit of a spontaneous, cultivated spirit.

Perfection comes from the very root of the well-nourished subconscious, and a little at random, like the flower.

The best art always gives a surprising, somewhat alien first impression, as absolute beauty would give. And then comes mutual conquest, and we are saved; the extraordinary makes *us* extraordinary.

In any work that is "complete," the perfect and the imperfect must exist in equilibrium, each with its perpetual, unavoidable, demanding, beautiful reality.

Perfect and imperfect, like the rose.

I like the defect. And I prefer to find it than to remove, diminish, or emend it. What I try to avoid is excess.

Defect—something like a verb ending or a declension, not immorality or ugliness.

Finding the defect is a matter of luck, as when you get something right. You don't search for it, you simply come upon it.

When perfection is impossible, search for character, which is almost always more, and never less, than perfection.

Poor lover of perfection, don't you see that you are a living poet and that life is undying imperfection?

What makes you perfect kills you. Without a doubt, perfection is poison.

The truly definitive is nothing but the exactly provisional.

Perfection is penultimate imperfection.

What a struggle between charm and perfection. Charming perfection, perfect charm.

Almost perfect: its greatest charm was in the "almost."

A quivering, restless perfection, whose ideal is normal imperfection.

A work of art is imperfect when, in form, the beautiful rushes ahead of the exact. Perfect when the exact and the beautiful coincide. But even better when the exact dominates the beautiful.

Perfection can only be successive.

One more step and we perish. The rose is like that.

I do not believe in perfection. I would believe in "impossible, successive perfection," as in "possible, successive imperfection . . ."

The perfect—that is, the complete—is always a never; I mean, the never of always.

Afterword

Afterword

. . . the never of always.

Did Juan Ramón succeed in his search for perfection?

He hoped to create a Book so perfectly beautiful that it would return the universe to silence and oneness. *One* book, his *Obra*, the Work to end all poetic work! He thought of that book as an ideal world and of himself as its god. Unlike the Maker he was emulating, he could not simply *will* that world into existence: "there is no way to perfection except through imperfection." He tried to believe that it would arise "successively," from the imperfection of life, out of the unitary rhythm of each day's work, led by instinct, refreshed by dream, helped by intelligence, and instructed by nature. What arose instead were *many* works—poems, prose, *books* of poems. When we consider those works, many seem perfect, and not merely as fragments. It is only when we remember the impossible goal he set for himself—the creation of that unitary Work—that we can say he did *not* succeed.

He was a victim of his own abundance, unable to gather all that he planted. He wrote tirelessly for more than six decades, and even with the help of Zenobia, who worked with him until a few days before she died, he was unable to "relive," revise, arrange, and publish all that he had saved of all that he had written. "Much and perfect. In the *and* lies the secret, the little problem." Or rather, the crux of his existence.

He was the god, not the savior, of his work.

Troubled by its abundance and diffuseness, he consoled himself with these words:

> I don't want people to read everything I have written. It is enough for some to read some things, and others other things, reading here and there. My passion is for my readers to be here and there in my work, but wherever their eyes rest, to find perfect beauty.

He searched for what is impossible either to write or to read — the perfect Work — and left, in his writing, an ardent defense of solitude and "invisible reality": dream and instinct, ecstasy and sorrow, gratitude and, above all, desire. We may say of him, using his own expression, that he "burned completely":

> In this world of ours we must burn completely. Each of us must resolve himself completely in the

flames, in the resolution that belongs to him alone. No Creator, no god that we can create could possibly accept those who do not fulfill their lives completely . . .

He "burned completely" in the flame of his daily work, pursuing, and not achieving, what he wanted. On the way to his impossible goal, he inspired others—his "immense minority"—to work, and to have faith in work. He found truths that mattered more than the goal. He discovered that "God is not the origin or the end, he is the middle"; that

the value of a work lies not in its end, in its "rounding off," but in the open, prickly spiritual and material vibration caused by its never-ending restlessness.

He liked beginnings and middles, not endings; odds, not evens. He liked sharp, pointy things rather than round ones (the aphorism is both). He discovered that poetry and perfection are always *becoming*, and came to accept that his own work was interminable "work in progress, imagination in movement, poetic succession." And perhaps this is his best lesson—the one he lived most intensely—about poetry, work, and perfection. He teaches that an impossible goal creates a possible path. It creates a present where we can "burn completely," holding nothing back, spending all of our strength on our *trabajo gustoso*, whatever it happens to be. In one of his earliest aphorisms, he wrote:

> The world does not need to come from a god. For better or worse, the world is here. But it does need to *go* to one (where is he?), and that is why the poet exists.

The poet leads us, forever, toward the mystery of perfection. Poetry, he wrote, is the "phenomenon that sets our being in motion." And so it is with perfection. It is never "had," never "realized" by anybody. It always escapes. By defending the impossible, the poet helps it to do so.

C.M.

Sources

This book, the theme, arrangement, and title of which are mine, draws on several works by Juan Ramón Jiménez. The aphorisms are taken from Antonio Sánchez Romeralo's splendid edition of *Ideolojía (1897–1957)* (Barcelona: Anthropos, 1990), which includes 4,116 of them and is used here by kind permission of Francisco H.-Pinzón Jiménez and the heirs of Juan Ramón Jiménez.

The aphorisms are presented in a different order than in Sánchez Romeralo, and this has made it necessary to omit some of Juan Ramón's titles. My own titles are in brackets. An ellipsis indicates an omission from the Spanish text.

There is no complete edition in Spanish of Juan Ramón's poetry. For a good selection, see Sánchez Romeralo's edition of *Poesías últimas escojidas (1918–1958)* (Madrid: Espasa-Calpe, 1982) (= *PUE*); his edition of *Leyenda (1896–1956)* (Madrid: Cupsa Editorial, 1978); and his clear and helpful introduction and notes to *La realidad invisible* (London: Tamesis Books, 1983).

There are fine translations of Jiménez's poetry by James Wright in *Above the River: The Complete Poems* (New York: Wesleyan University Press/ Farrar, Straus and Giroux/University Press of New England, 1990), pp. 87–90; and by Robert Bly, a steady defender of Jiménez's work since the 1960s, in *Forty Poems* (Madison, Minn.: Sixties Press, 1967). See also Robert Bly et al., tr., *Light and Shadows: Selected Poems and Prose* (Fredonia,

N.Y.: White Pine Press, 1987), and Robert Bly, *American Poetry: Wildness and Domesticity* (New York: Harper and Row, 1991). Antonio T. de Nicolas has published three volumes of Jiménez with prefaces by Louis Simpson: *Time and Space: A Poetic Autobiography*, *God Desired and Desiring*, and *Invisible Reality* (Paragon House, 1986–87). There is a recent translation by Myra C. Livingston and Joseph F. Domínguez of *Platero* (Boston: Houghton Mifflin, 1994).

On Juan Ramón's reading of English poetry, especially of Yeats, Blake, and Shelley, see Howard Young, *The Line in the Margin* (Madison: University of Wisconsin Press, 1980).

There is no thorough biography in English. The best one in Spanish is that of Graciela Palau de Nemes, *Vida y obra de JRJ: La poesía desnuda*, 2nd ed. (Madrid: Gredos, 1975). Juan Guerrero Ruiz's *Juan Ramón de viva voz* (Madrid: Insula, 1961) is an entertaining record of his daily conversation, 1913–36, by his "Boswell"; and the *Diario* of Juan Ramón's intelligent, lovely wife, Zenobia Camprubí, well edited and translated from English into Spanish by Graciela Palau de Nemes, vol. 1 (Madrid: Alianza/Universidad de Puerto Rico, 1991), gives a vivid picture of their life in exile. Recommended also is Ricardo Gullón, *El último Juan Ramón. Así se fueron los ríos* (Madrid: Alfaguara, 1968).

The notes that follow cover (1) works cited in the introduction and in the essays preceding each series of aphorisms; (2) sources of the poems translated here. The works are given in the order in which they are quoted. Juan Ramón Jiménez is abbreviated as JRJ.

Introduction (pp. 1–22)

"When I publish a book . . ." in JRJ, *Leyenda*, p. xiii. "How close to the soul . . ." in JRJ, *Tercera antología poética (1898–1953)* (Madrid: Biblioteca Nueva, 1957), p. 461; a later version appears in *Leyenda*, p. 401. "I dreamed for our language . . ." in JRJ, *Ideolojía*, p. 83. Aphorisms on Spain from *Ideolojía*, pp. 351–52 and 401. On Shelley: Young, *Line in the Margin*, p. 63. "Constant, endless fervor . . ." in *PUE*, p. 105. On JRJ and his disciples, *Lorca and Jiménez: Selected Poems*, tr. Robert Bly (Boston: Beacon Press, 1973), p. 3. On JRJ's plans for publishing his work, see Guerrero Ruiz, *Juan Ramón de viva voz*, passim. "I would like my book . . ." in JRJ, *Tercera antología poética*, p. 623. On "unwritten poetry," *Ideolojía*, pp. 461, 503. W. H. Auden, *The Dyer's Hand* (New York: Vintage, 1962), p. 67. On reading poetry, *Ideolojía*, p. 381. Rainer Maria Rilke, *Rodin*, tr. Robert Firmage (Salt Lake City: Peregrine Smith, 1979), p. 95.

Rhythm (pp. 35–47)

The Simone Weil Reader, ed. George A. Panichas (New York: David McKay, 1977), p. 61.

"That day . . ." in *PUE*, p. 171.

Silence (pp. 49–60)

On JRJ and Shakespeare, see Carmen Pérez Romero, *Juan Ramón Jiménez y la poesía anglosajona* (Cáceres: Universidad de Extremadura, 1992), p. 46. For the story of the cricket, Guerrero Ruiz, *Juan Ramón de viva voz*, p. 243.

JRJ: "El grillo real" ("The Real Cricket"), in *Por el cristal amarillo*, ed. Francisco Garfias (Madrid: Aguilar, 1961), pp. 191–92.

The Present (pp. 61–68)

Samuel Johnson, *Rambler* article, Tuesday, August 7, 1750, in *Works*, vol. 4, ed. Arthur Murphy (London: Joyce Gold, 1806), p. 239.

JRJ: "Take care of this Day . . ." in *Libros de poesía*, ed. Augustín Caballero (Madrid: Aguilar, 1959) p. 204; "Your strength . . ." in *PUE*, p. 102; "Light," in *PUE*, p. 102; "I awoke . . ." in *PUE*, p. 108.

Memory (pp. 69–77)

JRJ: "Oh secret memories . . ." in *PUE*, p. 888; "How sad . . ." in *PUE*, 104; "Oh time . . ." in *PUE*, p. 888.

Idealism (pp. 79–88)

Sir Philip Sidney, *An Apology for Poetry*, ed. Forrest G. Robinson (New York: Macmillan, 1986), pp. 17, 22. Francis Bacon, *Essays Civil and Moral, The Advancement of Learning, Novum Organum, Etc.* (London, Ward, Lock, s.a.), p. 154.

JRJ: *Por el cristal amarillo*, p. 175.

Nature (pp. 89–103)

Sidney, *Apology*, p. 17. Ralph Waldo Emerson, "The Poet," in *Essays*, ed. Irwin Edman (New York: Crowell, 1926), pp. 278, 398. Rilke, *Rodin*, p. 96. Bill McKibben, *The End of Nature* (New York: Random House, 1989). Emerson, "Nature," in *Essays*, p. 398.

JRJ: "This is my life . . ." in *PUE*, p. 90; "White cloud . . ." in *PUE*, p. 82.

Instinct (pp. 105–13)

William Morris, quoted in Carl Fehrman, *Poetic Creation: Inspiration or Craft*, tr. Karin Petherick (Minneapolis: University of Minnesota, 1980), p. 75. Edgar Allan Poe, *Complete Works*, ed. James A. Harrison (New York: Crowell, 1902), vol. 14, p. 195. Paul Valéry, "I seek a word . . ." in Fehrman, *Poetic Creation*, p. 87. Lorca, *Deep Song and Other Prose*, p. 44. Rilke, *Rodin*, p. 89.

Dream (pp. 115–28)

Bly, *American Poetry*, p. 5. Gaston Bachelard, *The Poetics of Reverie. Childhood, Language, and the Cosmos*, tr. Daniel Russell (Boston: Beacon Press, 1971), p. 145.

JRJ: "The poem calls to me . . ." in *Tiempo y Espacio*, ed. Arturo del Villar (Madrid: EDAF, 1986), p. 168; "There is a me . . ." in *PUE*, 158; "Riches of night . . ." in *Leyenda*, p. 786; "How very sad . . . !" in *Tiempo y Espacio*, p. 166; "For you, life . . ." in *Libros de poesía*, p. 736; "Sleepless," in *PUE*, p. 82; "Above and Below Our Death," in *Tiempo y Espacio*, p. 169.

Death (pp. 129–39)

Miguel de Unamuno, *Del sentimiento trágico de la vida* (Madrid: Alianza, 1986), p. 252. Guerrero Ruiz, *Juan Ramón de viva voz*, p. 329. Lorca, *Deep Song and Other Prose*, pp. 44, 50. Francisco de Quevedo, *Obra poética*, ed. José Manuel Blecua (Madrid: Editorial Castalia, 1989), pp. 184–85.

JRJ: "Work," in *Realidad invisible*, p. 95; "Light and Shadow," in *Leyenda*, p. 517; "Death is an old mother . . ." in *PUE*, pp. 152–53; "Ah, sleep . . ." in *PUE*, p. 146; "What happens . . ." in *PUE*, p. 148.

Writing (pp. 141–53)

There is a phonograph recording of JRJ reading another version of the poem by Abū Saʻīd ibn Abi ʻl-Khair: *Archivo de la Palabra* (Madrid: Publicaciones de la Residencia de Estudiantes). On "literature" and "poetry": JRJ, *Política poética* (Madrid: Alianza Editorial, 1982), p. 83. Unamuno, *Del sentimiento trágico*, p. 253.

JRJ: "This or that person says to me . . ." in *Ideolojía*, p. 192; "Intelligence, give me . . ." in *Leyenda*, p. 422.

Revision (pp. 155–69)

Gaston Bachelard, *The Psychoanalysis of Fire*, tr. Alan C. M. Ross (Boston: Beacon Press, 1964), pp. 30–31. Guerrero Ruiz, *Juan Ramón de viva voz*, p. 131.

JRJ: "Touch it no more . . ." in *Leyenda*, p. 449.